W9-BTT-962

New Classics

Kraft Kitchens

New Classics
Our most requested recipes made simple

Clarkson Potter/Publishers
New York

Published by Clarkson Potter/Publishers, New York.
Member of the Crown Publishing Group, a division of Random House, Inc.
www.randomhouse.com

CLARKSON N. POTTER is a trademark and POTTER and colophon are registered trademarks
of Random House, Inc.

Printed in Canada

Design by: Vicki Hornsby
Cover photography by: MIchael Kohn

Library of Congress Cataloguing-in-Publication Data
Kraft Kitchens new classics : our most requested recipes made simple
       p. cm
    1. Quick and easy cookery. I. Title: New classics. II. Kraft Kitchens.
TX833.5 .K73 2002
641.5'55-dc21   2002151009

ISBN 0-609-81048-0

10 9 8 7 6 5 4 3 2 1

First Edition

Cover: Everyday Easy Lasagna, page 58. Previous page: From an ad for Velveeta, 1938.

The following brands are a part of the Kraft family of tasty and convenient products. In many of the recipes in this book, you'll find shortened references to them. Their full names are given here to help you when you shop:

BAKER'S Semi-Sweet Baking Chocolate
BAKER'S Semi-Sweet Chocolate Chunks
BAKER'S Unsweetened Baking
   Chocolate
CHEEZ WHIZ Cheese Dip
COOL WHIP Whipped Topping
HONEY MAID Honey Grahams
JELL-O Chocolate Flavor Instant
   Pudding & Pie Filling
JELL-O Gelatin
JELL-O Pistachio Flavor Instant
   Pudding & Pie Filling
JELL-O Vanilla Flavor Instant
   Pudding & Pie Filling
KRAFT Barbecue Sauce
KRAFT CATALINA Dressing
KRAFT Classic Caesar Dressing
KRAFT Deluxe Macaroni & Cheese
   Dinner
KRAFT Dressing
KRAFT Italian Style Shredded Cheese
KRAFT LIGHT DONE RIGHT Classic
   Caesar Reduced Fat Dressing
KRAFT LIGHT DONE RIGHT Italian
   Reduced Fat Dressing

KRAFT Macaroni & Cheese Dinner
KRAFT Mayo Real Mayonnaise
KRAFT Mexican Style Shredded
   Cheese
KRAFT 100% Grated Parmesan
   Cheese
KRAFT Peppercorn Ranch Dressing
KRAFT Ranch Dressing
KRAFT Shredded Cheddar Cheese
KRAFT Shredded Cheese
KRAFT Shredded Mozzarella Cheese
KRAFT Singles
KRAFT Swiss Cheese
MINUTE White Rice
MIRACLE WHIP LIGHT Dressing
MIRACLE WHIP Salad Dressing
NILLA Wafers
OREO Chocolate Sandwich Cookies
PHILADELPHIA Chive & Onion Cream
   Cheese Spread
PHILADELPHIA Cream Cheese
PHILADELPHIA Cream Cheese
   Spread
PHILADELPHIA Light Cream Cheese
   Spread

PHILADELPHIA Light Roasted Garlic
   Cream Cheese Spread
PHILADELPHIA Pineapple Cream
   Cheese Spread
PHILADELPHIA Strawberry Cream
   Cheese Spread
POST ALPHA-BITS Frosted
   Letter Shaped Oat and Corn Cereal
POST Cocoa PEBBLES Cereal
POST GOLDEN CRISPS Sweetened
   Puffed Wheat Cereal
POST HONEY BUNCHES OF OATS Cereal
POST 100% Bran Cereal
POST Raisin Bran Cereal
POST SPOON SIZE Shredded Wheat
   Cereal
Raspberry FIG NEWTONS Fruit
   Chewy Cookies
RITZ Crackers
SHAKE'N BAKE Seasoned Coating Mix
STOVE TOP Stuffing Mix
STOVE TOP Stuffing Mix for Chicken
VELVEETA Pasteurized Prepared
   Cheese Product
VELVEETA Shells & Cheese Dinner

Contents

From an ad for Ritz Crackers, mid-1950s.

At the Kraft Kitchens

Here are the people who helped bring you the book you are holding right now:

Recipe Content Team
Cécile Girard-Hicks, Stephanie Williams, Lorna Roberts, Tracy Sherva, Michele McAdoo, Susanne Stark

Recipe Development
Karen Didier, Lisa Brandt-Whittington, Marla Goldberg, Maxine Karpel, Kathleen Mackintosh, Cayla Runka

Recipe Editor
Betty Heinlen

Marketing Team
Maureen Weiss, Gretchen Claus Hickman, Gillian Fripp, Carol Blindauer, Lori Sugarman

Photography
All photography produced by Michael Kohn, photographer; Sue Henderson, food stylist; Catherine MacFadyen, prop stylist; Vicki Hornsby, art director; Ashley Denton, food-styling assistant; Shelagh McAuliffe, photography assistant; except for that which appears on pages 16, 91, 100, by Gibson and Smith; 19, by Michael Alberstat; 60, by Edward Pond; and 76, by Andreas Trauttmansdorff.

Dedicated to all of you, your friends and family,
who have shared our recipes at your tables and made them Classics.

Introduction
100 YEARS OF GREAT CLASSIC TASTES

Think back to your childhood and you may realize that many of your fondest recollections are linked to gatherings of relatives and friends – and to the much-loved family standards that drew you to the table on those special occasions. Maybe it was a favorite cheesecake for Dad's birthday or your grandmother's potato salad at an annual summer barbecue? Even as times change, the value of such traditions stays as strong as ever.

For 100 years, Kraft has helped families like yours to create happy memories involving food. When you needed an easier way to prepare a fresh salad we were there with Miracle Whip, mayonnaise and a host of bottled dressings. When you wanted to get lunch and dinner on the table faster, our Deluxe Process Cheese Slices and Macaroni & Cheese Dinner – groundbreaking products in their time – were there for you. So it continues, as we commit ourselves to helping nurture your family's food memories in the years ahead.

New Classics is the direct result of letters, e-mails and phone calls from many of you, telling us about your favorite Kraft recipes: We listened and we learned, and now we've gathered these most requested and popular recipes into one terrific book to share with family and friends. What exactly is a New Classic? It's a time-honored favorite recipe – yours, your mother's or even your grandmother's – made easier than ever to prepare. That's why we're so sure you'll enjoy every one of these dishes, in the cookbook you helped us to create.

In 1905, a charming child enhanced the Jell-O image as a "dainty dessert." Seventy-five years later, the look was a little more informal (opposite) when it came to Kool-Aid and kids.

Modern lines, 1920s style, marked the design of the first Kraft Kitchen. Kraft offers new choices for the cheese tray (below) and a range of handy cheese-based recipes for eager cooks everywhere. By 1943, the mood was enterprising and solidly patriotic – as in this magazine advertisement for Miracle Whip (right).

Our family tree: A century of classic recipes

Just as the chapters of your family's history go on from generation to generation, Kraft's family of brands has its own history, chronicled in an ever-growing legacy of classic recipes.

In 1903, James Lewis Kraft traveled to Chicago, Illinois, in the U.S., from Fort Erie, Ontario, in Canada. With him, he brought $65, a horse-drawn wagon, the ability to work hard, a knowledge of food and marketing and the determination to build a solid business. Over time, his company grew from a one-man operation into the diverse international organization of today.

At about the same time, Jell-O Brand Gelatin, which later joined the Kraft family of products, was designated "America's Most Famous Dessert" and home economists were called upon to provide helpful tips and new uses of this product for enthusiastic consumers. Still as popular today, Jell-O molded desserts and salads have become true North American classics.

By the 1920s, home cooks everywhere wanted more information about Kraft's expanding family of products. And so the Kraft Kitchens were born. Early kitchen work focused on the needs of cooks at that time, resulting in

innovative recipes featuring cheese in its new, packaged form. Classics that everyone clamored for included toasted cheese sandwiches and macaroni and cheese (see page 66).

As our soldiers marched off to World War II, food shortages and rationing shifted the Kraft Kitchens into high gear. We worked hard to develop dependable, pleasing recipes that met ration requirements. By doing so, we enabled families to enjoy favorite dishes at a time when comfort foods were particularly meaningful. (See Ritz Mock Apple Pie, page 111.) One innovative Kraft classic recipe for chocolate cake even used Miracle Whip Salad Dressing in place of oil. (See Heavenly Chocolate Cake, page 119.)

When television hit the airwaves at the end of the 1940s, it provided yet another way for us to

The mood was lively in the decades that followed the end of World War II. In 1961, Kraft Barbecue Sauce (right) was a barbecue essential, and salads were better than ever (below) with Good Seasons Salad Dressing Mix.

share food ideas and techniques. Radio cooking shows now made way for televised food specialists, who prepared enticing recipes before viewers' eyes. The power of this new medium was highlighted dramatically with the airing of a Philadelphia Cream Cheese recipe for trendy clam dip: The television spot caused shortages of canned clams in grocery stores along the entire Eastern seaboard of the United States. (See Classic Clam Dip, page 14.)

During the '60s and '70s, the Kraft Kitchens responded to the new demand for time-saving recipes. As more women entered the work force, we devised quicker recipes to put home-cooked family meals on the table with less time and effort. Recipes featuring convenience ingredients, such as Minute White Rice and Cool Whip Whipped Topping, were among these new classics. We also developed speedy kitchen tips — such as softening cream cheese or melting chocolate in a microwave oven — to share with our consumers.

When fitness and health took the spotlight in the

New Kraft Barbecue Sauce simmers real cook-out flavor right into the meat!

When it starts to simmer, the flavor really speaks up. This is the barbecue sauce that gives you the flavor you cook outdoors to get. The Kraft cooks made it that way—with nineteen herbs and spices. And once it's on the fire, those simmering spice flavors seep right in and keep the meat juicy. Try new Kraft Barbecue Sauce in your kitchen, too; cooks who do say that it brings its real cook-out flavor right indoors—and what could be better than that?

'80s and '90s, many of Kraft's favorite recipes were revised to accommodate the desire for wider dietary choice. And reduced-calorie, sugar-free or reduced-fat versions of food favorites such as Kraft Dressings and Kraft cheese were introduced.

Our families today: The dawn of a new century

The twenty-first century is here, and as *New Classics* illustrates, Kraft is already attuned to your family's present needs. Busy lifestyles have gotten busier, and so our quick classic recipes take even less time than before. Because a generation raised on salsa craves intense flavors, we've updated familiar recipes with zesty new ingredients, as well.

Despite all the changes, one classic concept stays the same – the importance of gathering around a table with loved ones to share delicious home cooking. So open this book and create some memorable moments of your very own to enjoy with those you hold dear. And remember to keep in touch with us. Thanks to you, tomorrow's newest classic may be just around the corner.

Brand new in the 1960s – revolutionary Cool Whip Whipped Topping (left); and in the 1970s, Kraft Singles made their mark (below).

MAKING YOUR EVERYDAY COOKING EASIER

It's easiest for us to explain the process by comparing the method we once used to explain a recipe (we'll use a stir-fry here) with the way we approach the same dish today.

Twenty years ago, our method of putting together a chicken stir-fry was a traditional one that looked pretty much like this:

CHICKEN STIR-FRY

4 medium-sized boneless
    chicken breasts, cut into strips
2 tbsp oil
1 cup celery, thinly sliced
1 medium green pepper, cut
    into strips
1 small onion, sliced
1 tsp salt

¼ tsp ground ginger
2 ½ cups bean sprouts
1 can water chestnuts, drained
    and sliced
½ cup chicken broth
2 tbsp soy sauce
2 tbsp cornstarch

Add chicken to hot oil in a large skillet and stir-fry for 2 to 3 minutes. Add celery, green pepper, onion, salt and ginger; stir-fry until vegetables are tender-crisp. Add bean sprouts, water chestnuts and chicken broth. Combine soy sauce and cornstarch; mix until smooth. Gradually stir soy mixture into chicken-broth mixture and cook, stirring constantly, until sauce is thickened. Serve over prepared rice. Serves 4.

When we thought about it, that traditional stir-fry seemed like a lot of work. It was, after all, just some meat, vegetables and sauce, served over rice.

So we began to undo the process, replacing 5 separate measured ingredients (and the inescapable challenge of keeping the cornstarch from lumping) with a splash of flavorful salad dressing as the foundation of our sauce. A few minor ingredients – like those water chestnuts – got lost along the way and we focused on the easy-to-grasp rules of thumb that would always work: a pound of meat for 4 people and a handful of each of the vegetables per person. We'd leave it up to you to cover a pan or leave it uncovered (although if it was important to do one or the other, we'd be sure to tell you).

And suddenly our stir-fry wasn't so complicated. In fact, with that stir-fry we were able to take the whole process down to 3 simple steps: starting the meat on its own; adding vegetables to the skillet partway through; then finishing the dish with some dressing to make the sauce.

Here's the result. With our recipes we utilize easy-to-follow 4-color grids – which show 4 tasty combinations of popular meat, vegetables and flavorings – to get you started. After you've practiced our approach it really becomes exciting, as you use the same simple process to mix and match ingredients to perfectly satisfy your own family's tastes.

THE SIMPLE STIR-FRY

Just follow our 3 simple steps:

1 STIR-FRY sliced **meat** (1 lb should do it for 4) with a bit of Kraft **dressing** for 10 minutes.

2 ADD sliced **veggies** (a handful per person) and cook 10 minutes more.

3 STIR in an additional ½ cup dressing to make a sauce. Serve over prepared rice.

And use the ingredients you have on hand …

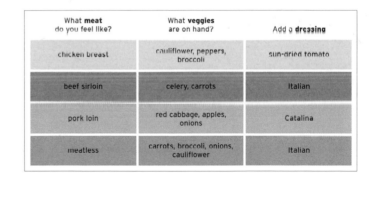

What **meat** do you feel like?	What **veggies** are on hand?	Add a **dressing**
chicken breast	cauliflower, peppers, broccoli	sun-dried tomato
beef sirloin	celery, carrots	Italian
pork loin	red cabbage, apples, onions	Catalina
meatless	carrots, broccoli, onions, cauliflower	Italian

We're Here to Help You

If you need help, just give us a call or send an e-mail.

Not every cookbook comes with a helpline, but ours does. Here in the Kraft Kitchens we listen to you and we're here to help with your cooking needs. Monday to Friday, 9 a.m. to 9 p.m. EST, you can call our helpline.

Our websites also provide additional classic recipes, all sorts of terrific dinner solutions, cooking tips and holiday ideas.

Whatever the method, we hope you will be in touch. We'd love to hear from you, whenever you have the time.

IN CANADA
HELPLINE
1-800-567-KRAFT
(9 a.m. to 9 p.m. EST,
Monday to Friday)
E-MAIL
kraftkitchens@kraft.com
WEBSITE

kraftcanada.com

IN THE UNITED STATES
HELPLINE
1-877-572-3843 (toll-free)
(9 a.m. to 9 p.m. EST,
Monday to Friday)
E-MAIL
classics@kraftfoods.com
WEBSITE

kraftfoods.com

First impressions should always be memorable, especially when they involve the food you put on your table. That welcome snack at the end of a busy afternoon, the flavorful dish that marks the start of a family dinner or the irresistible plate of goodies set out for an evening at home doesn't have to be complicated or time-consuming to prepare. It simply has to taste delicious. If it looks appealing

Starters & Soups

and its smells are enticing even better, of course – because anticipation is such a big part of the pleasure. And that's the focus of every easy Kraft Kitchens recipe you'll find in the pages that follow. We've taken many of your favorite snack mixes, savory finger foods, luscious dips and heartwarming soups, featuring time-tested combinations of ingredients we know you love, and we've made them easier and better tasting than ever before. Which is why we're sure you're going to enjoy every one of these recipes and why we think of them as true New Classics.

THE ORIGINAL MUNCH MIX

Just follow our 3 simple steps:
1 PLACE 4 cups Post Spoon Size Shredded Wheat Cereal, 2 cups popped popcorn, 1 cup small pretzels and 1 cup mixed nuts or peanuts in 15- x 10- x 1-inch baking pan. Sprinkle evenly with 1 envelope Italian salad dressing mix.
2 MIX ¼ cup butter or margarine, melted, 2 tablespoons Worcestershire sauce and ¼ teaspoon garlic powder. Drizzle evenly over cereal mixture; stir to coat.
3 BAKE at 300°F for 30–35 minutes or until crisp, stirring halfway through baking time. Cool. Store in tightly covered container up to 1 week.

>> KRAFT KITCHENS TIP
After Munch Mix has cooled, have the kids spoon 2-cup portions into small plastic bags and tie with colorful holiday ribbons. Give these gifts to the mailman, crossing guard or anyone else who makes a difference in your life.

CRUNCHY PARMESAN POPCORN

Just follow our 3 simple steps:
1 MIX 12 cups hot, unsalted popped popcorn (⅓ cup, unpopped) with ⅓ cup *each* butter or margarine and grated Parmesan cheese; toss lightly until well coated.
2 SPREAD in single layer on baking sheet.
3 BAKE at 375°F for 5–7 minutes or until golden brown.

10-MINUTE APPETIZER DIPS

>> TRY THIS, TOO
For a great substitute, use Philadelphia Light Cream Cheese Spread and Miracle Whip Light.

>> CLASSIC CLAM DIP
Mix 1 can (6-½ oz) minced clams, 1 package (8 oz) Philadelphia Cream Cheese, softened, 2 teaspoons lemon juice, 1-½ teaspoons Worcestershire sauce and ¼ teaspoon garlic salt. Serve with potato chips.

Just follow our 3 simple steps:

1 MIX 1 package (8 oz) Philadelphia Cream Cheese, softened, with ½ cup Miracle Whip. Spread mixture on pie plate or serving platter.

2 LAYER sliced/chopped **toppings** on base.

3 SPRINKLE with **Kraft Shredded Cheese**. Serve with pita bread, crackers, tortilla chips and fresh veggies.

And use the ingredients you have on hand …

What **toppings** do you have on hand?	And finish with **Kraft Shredded Cheese**
salsa, tomatoes, shredded lettuce	Mexican Style
tomatoes, cucumbers, black olives	Mozzarella
pesto, artichokes, grilled eggplant and peppers	Italian Style
pasta or pizza sauce, pepperoni, peppers	Italian Style

HOT DIPS

SWISS ALMOND DIP

Just follow our 2 simple steps:

1 MIX in pie plate or ovenproof serving dish, 1 package (8 oz) cream cheese, softened, 1-½ cups shredded Kraft Swiss Cheese, ⅓ cup *each* mayonnaise and chopped green onions.

2 BAKE at 350°F for 15 minutes, stirring once during baking. Top with slivered almonds. Serve warm with pita crisps, baguette slices, broccoli, cauliflower and asparagus.

ARTICHOKE DIP

Just follow our 2 simple steps:

1 MIX in a pie plate or ovenproof dish, 1 cup *each* mayonnaise and Kraft 100% Grated Parmesan Cheese, with 1 can (14 oz) artichoke hearts, drained and chopped.

2 BAKE at 350°F for 15 minutes or until dip is hot and bubbly. Serve with assorted dippers such as vegetables and crackers.

CHILI-CHEESE DIP

Just follow our 3 simple steps:

1 SPREAD 1 package (8 oz) cream cheese, softened, on bottom of microwavable pie plate.

2 TOP with 1 can (15 oz) chili; sprinkle with shredded Cheddar cheese.

3 MICROWAVE on HIGH 3 minutes or until thoroughly heated. Serve warm with tortilla chips.

>> **TRY THIS, TOO**
Sprinkle Chili-Cheese Dip with ½ cup *each* chopped onion and chopped green pepper before topping with chili and cheese.

>> **VELVEETA SALSA DIP**
Cube 1 lb Velveeta and mix with 1 cup salsa in a microwavable bowl. Microwave on HIGH for 5 minutes or until melted, stirring after 2 minutes.

FRESH TOMATO-AND-HERB BRUSCHETTA

>> KRAFT KITCHENS TIP
To seed tomatoes, cut in
half crosswise and gently
squeeze out seeds
over sink or use a spoon
to scoop out seeds.

Just follow our 2 simple steps:
1 SLICE French bread into thick slices and grill until golden.
2 MIX 4 large tomatoes, seeded and chopped, several spoonfuls of sun-dried
tomato vinaigrette dressing and a handful of shredded Italian-style cheese
in small bowl. Serve tomato mixture with grilled bread.

DEVILED EGGS

Just follow our 3 simple steps:
1 CUT 6 hard-cooked eggs in half lengthwise; remove yolks.
2 MIX yolks with ⅓ cup Miracle Whip.
3 SPOON yolk mixture into egg whites; sprinkle with paprika.

SHAKE'N BAKE CHICKEN FINGERS

Just follow our 2 simple steps:
1 CUT 5-6 boneless, skinless chicken breasts into strips. Coat with Shake'N
Bake Original Coating Mix as directed on package.
2 BAKE at 400°F for 10 minutes or until cooked through. Serve with
barbecue sauce, salsa or honey as a dip.

4 WAYS WITH NACHOS

Just follow our 3 simple steps:

1 PLACE a layer of **tortilla chips** or **crackers** in baking dish.

2 MIX 2 cups **shredded cheese** and **add-ins** in bowl; spread half evenly over nachos. Repeat layers, ending with topping layer.

3 BAKE at 400°F for 8–10 minutes or until cheese melts.

And use the ingredients you have on hand …

What **tortilla chips** or **crackers** do you want?	Use this **shredded cheese**	Try these **add-ins**
blue tortilla chips	Mexican-style	diced cooked chicken, tomatoes and Jalapeño peppers
tortilla chips, triangular	Cheddar	diced tomatoes, frozen corn, kidney beans and chili powder
whole-wheat crackers	Italian-style	diced tomatoes, zucchini, black olives and dash of oregano
snack crackers	mozzarella	strips of pepper, garlic powder and dash of oregano

Blue Nachos with Chicken, Tomatoes and Jalapeño Peppers

MANHATTAN MEATBALLS

>> **KRAFT KITCHENS TIP**
Meatballs cook evenly
when they are all the same
size. Use a small ice-cream
scoop or scant ¼ cup
measuring cup to portion
even amounts of meat.

Just follow our 3 simple steps:

1 MIX 2 lb ground **meat**, 1 cup dry seasoned bread crumbs and 2 eggs. Shape into 1-inch meatballs, placing on foil-lined 15- x 10- x 1-inch baking pan.

2 MIX 1 cup Kraft Original Barbecue Sauce, 1 jar (12 oz) **jelly or preserves** and a spoonful of **seasoning**. Pour over meatballs.

3 BAKE at 375°F for 40 minutes, stirring halfway through cooking.

And use the ingredients you have on hand …

What ground **meat** do you feel like?	Which **jelly or preserves** do you have on hand?	And now for the **seasoning**
turkey	peach preserves	ground ginger
beef	grape jelly	black pepper
pork	apricot preserves	soy sauce
pork sausage	orange marmalade	hot pepper flakes

Manhattan Beef Meatballs

MANHATTAN CLAM CHOWDER

Just follow our 3 simple steps:
1 DRAIN 2 cans (6-½ oz *each*) minced clams, reserving liquid. Add enough water to reserved liquid to measure 3 cups.
2 SIMMER clam juice/water mixture, 1 can (16 oz) undrained diced tomatoes, ½ cup *each* chopped onion and carrot, 2 potatoes, peeled and cubed, and ½ teaspoon dried thyme in large covered saucepan for 30 minutes.
3 REMOVE from heat and mash vegetables slightly to thicken broth. Stir in minced clams. Heat thoroughly. Season to taste with salt and pepper.

NEW ENGLAND CLAM CHOWDER

Just follow our 3 simple steps:
1 COOK 4 slices bacon in medium saucepan until crisp; drain and set aside, reserving 2 tablespoons bacon drippings.
2 SAUTÉ 2 potatoes, peeled and cubed, and ¼ cup *each* chopped carrot, onion and celery in reserved bacon drippings until tender.
3 STIR in 1 tub (8 oz) cream cheese spread, 2 cans (6-½ oz *each*) minced clams with juice, cooked bacon, 2 cups milk and 1 cup water. Simmer 15-20 minutes.

SMOOTH & CREAMY VEGETABLE SOUPS

>> KRAFT KITCHENS TIP
For a healthful alternative
to traditional cream
soups, we've thickened
our version with a puree
of rice and vegetables
in place of heavy cream.

Just follow our 3 simple steps:

1 MIX 1 *each* onion, carrot and celery stalk, chopped, in large pot with 2 cans (10-½ oz *each*) condensed chicken broth and 3 cans water. Bring to boil. Cook 5-10 minutes or until tender.
2 ADD 4 cups chopped **veggies**, ½ cup uncooked Minute White Rice, salt and pepper to taste and 1-2 teaspoons **spices**. Cook on medium heat 10-15 minutes or until veggies are tender. Pour in 1 can milk.
3 PURÉE soup in batches, in a blender or food processor, return to pot and gently heat on low until warm.

And use the ingredients you have on hand …

What **veggies** do you feel like?	Now for the **spices**
broccoli	chili powder
cauliflower	curry powder
carrots	ground ginger
peeled butternut squash	ground nutmeg

Creamy Cauliflower Soup

FRENCH ONION SOUP

Just follow our 3 simple steps:
1 PLACE 3 large Spanish onions, sliced, 1 can (10-½ oz) condensed beef broth, 1 can water and 1 bay leaf in large pot. Bring to a boil, reduce heat and simmer 25 minutes.
2 REMOVE bay leaf and divide into 6 ovenproof bowls, topping each bowl with slice of toasted French bread.
3 COMBINE shredded Swiss, mozzarella and Parmesan cheese. Sprinkle each bowl with a handful of cheese. Broil 5-10 minutes or until cheese melts.

CHEESY BROCCOLI SOUP

Just follow our 3 simple steps:
1 COOK 1 large bunch broccoli, chopped, and 2 carrots, chopped, in saucepan with 1 can (10-½ oz) condensed chicken broth and 1 can water until tender. Let cool 10 minutes.
2 POUR into blender; cover. Process until smooth; return to saucepan.
3 WHISK in ½ cup milk and 1 cup Cheez Whiz on low heat. Do not allow to boil.

A century is a long time, and over the past 100 years we've made an interesting and diverse assortment of delicious salads and other vegetable dishes. In many instances, their styles directly reflect the time of their invention. Some of these mealtime standards have been with us for years and years, and yet the best of them still seem as fresh and right as they were the very first time they

Salads & Sides

were served. All they need is a minor touch or two to make them seem an absolutely perfect fit for modern-day sensibilities and tastes. We love the names of them – Waldorf and Cobb salads, for example, and old-fashioned Corn Pudding. We also love the memories they evoke, of family reunions, community suppers, school picnics or summertime company celebrations. We think you'll be more than happy to remember such old favorites, especially when you discover that these recipes make them easier and better-tasting than they've ever been before.

CREATE A COLESLAW

Just follow our 2 simple steps:
1 POUR 1 package shredded-coleslaw mix into large bowl.
2 TOSS with creamy coleslaw dressing and an add-in or two, if you like.

Choose from these add-ins:

1 can (11 oz) of mandarin-orange segments, drained; chopped red and green apples; handful of bacon bits; horseradish; nuts and raisins; pickle relish; shredded carrot; 1 cup crushed pineapple; spoonful of dill; spoonful of mustard.

TANGY BROCCOLI SALAD

Just follow our 2 simple steps:
1 MIX 1 cup Miracle Whip or Miracle Whip Light and 2 tablespoons *each* sugar and vinegar in large bowl.
2 ADD 1 medium bunch broccoli, cut into florets (about 6 cups), a handful of bacon bits and ⅓ medium red onion, chopped. Cover. Refrigerate until ready to serve.

>> **INSIDE A CLASSIC**
In the 1930s, Kraft introduced Miracle Whip Salad Dressing – a product that combined the best features of mayonnaise and old-fashioned boiled dressing. For the first time, salads began to be served regularly in homes throughout North America.

WALDORF SALAD

>> KRAFT KITCHENS TIP
For optimum flavor, use tart apples, such as Granny Smiths, in this classic Waldorf Salad recipe.

Toss 3 cups coarsely chopped apples, 1 cup sliced celery and ½ cup *each* Kraft Mayo and coarsely chopped walnuts. Cover. Refrigerate until ready to serve. Serve in lettuce-lined bowl, if desired.

Also try one of these add-ins:

Chopped cooked chicken or turkey; chopped dates; halved seedless green grapes; miniature marshmallows; raisins or toasted coconut.

WATERGATE SALAD

Just follow our 3 simple steps:

1 MIX 1 package (4-serving size) Jell-O Pistachio Flavor Instant Pudding & Pie Filling, 1 can (20 oz) crushed pineapple with juice, 1 cup miniature marshmallows and ½ cup chopped pecans in large bowl until well blended.

2 ADD 2 cups thawed whipped topping; stir gently. Cover. Refrigerate 1 hour or until ready to serve.

3 TOP with additional whipped topping and sliced strawberries just before serving, if desired.

5-CUP SALAD

Just follow our 2 simple steps:
1 TOSS 1 can (11 oz) mandarin orange segments, drained, 1 cup *each* pineapple chunks, coconut, miniature marshmallows and sour cream. Cover.
2 REFRIGERATE several hours or until chilled.

COBB SALAD

Just follow our 3 simple steps:
1 ARRANGE 6 cups torn mixed salad greens, 2 cups chopped deli turkey slices, 2 tomatoes, chopped, 2 hard-cooked eggs, chopped, and 1 avocado, peeled and chopped, on large serving platter.
2 SPRINKLE 6 slices bacon, crisply cooked and crumbled, and 2 cups shredded Cheddar cheese over top.
3 DRIZZLE with French dressing. Sprinkle with crumbled blue cheese, if desired.

>> TRY THIS, TOO Cobb Salad is also great with ranch dressing.

>> KRAFT KITCHENS TIP
For a more interesting texture, try toasting the coconut in 5-Cup Salad.

Thinly spread coconut on baking sheet. Bake at 350°F for 7-12 minutes, stirring occasionally, until lightly browned.

POTATO SALAD

>> KRAFT KITCHENS TIP
Red-skinned or new potatoes are recommended for use in this salad. They cube neatly after boiling and they easily absorb the dressing, too.

Miracle Whip Light or reduced-fat sour cream are both great dressing substitutes.

Just follow our 3 simple steps:

1 MIX ¾ cup **dressing** and a spoonful of **seasonings** in large bowl.

2 ADD 6 cups cubed cooked potatoes (about 2 lb) and chopped **add-ins** (a handful of *each* should do it); mix lightly. Cover.

3 REFRIGERATE several hours or until chilled.

And use the ingredients you have on hand …

What **dressing** do you feel like?	Try these **seasonings**	And now for the **add-ins**
Miracle Whip or mayonnaise	Dijon mustard	celery, hard-cooked eggs and sweet pickle relish
sour cream	chopped fresh dill	cucumber, hard-cooked eggs and red onion
Italian	minced garlic	feta cheese, green pepper and red onion
ranch	chopped cilantro	corn, red or green pepper and canned green chilies

Potato Salad with Celery, Hard-Cooked Eggs and Sweet Pickle Relish

CLASSIC GREEK SALAD

Just follow our 2 simple steps:
1 MIX 3 tomatoes, chopped, 1 cucumber, sliced, and ½ cup *each* thinly sliced red onion and whole ripe Kalamata olives in large bowl.
2 TOSS with 1 cup crumbled feta cheese and ½ cup Greek vinaigrette dressing.

TACO SALAD

Just follow our 3 simple steps:
1 BROWN 1 lb ground beef; drain. Add 1 package (1-¼ oz) taco-seasoning mix; prepare as directed on package.
2 PLACE shredded iceberg lettuce in large serving bowl; cover with layers of ground beef mixture, Kraft Shredded Cheddar Cheese and tomato wedges.
3 TOP with pitted black olives, crushed tortilla chips, salsa and sour cream.

>> TRY THIS, TOO
Serve prepared Greek Salad ingredients over torn romaine or iceberg lettuce. Or serve with toasted pita bread wedges.

You can also substitute Italian reduced-fat dressing for Greek vinaigrette dressing in this Greek Salad.

CAESAR SALAD

>> TRY THIS, TOO
You can also substitute
Kraft Caesar Reduced Fat
Dressing for regular
dressing in this Caesar
Salad.

>> CHICKEN CAESAR SALAD
Toss 2 cups cooked chicken
strips with other salad
ingredients. Add additional
dressing, if desired.

TOSS 8 cups torn romaine lettuce, 1 cup seasoned croutons and ½ cup *each* shredded Parmesan cheese and Kraft Caesar Dressing in large salad bowl. Serve immediately.

SPINACH SALAD

Just follow our 3 simple steps:
1 TOSS 2 packages (10 oz *each*) fresh baby spinach in large bowl with ½ small red onion, sliced, 4 hard-cooked eggs, chopped, and 1 cup sliced fresh mushrooms.
2 MICROWAVE ½ cup Italian dressing in microwavable measuring cup on HIGH for 20 seconds. Drizzle over salad; toss lightly.
3 SPRINKLE with bacon bits.

EVERYDAY EASY RICE SALADS

Just follow our 3 simple steps:

1 TOSS 4 cups cooked Minute White Rice with a few handfuls of chopped **veggies/fruit**.

2 MIX 1 cup Miracle Whip or Miracle Whip Light with **juice/peel** and **seasonings**.

3 ADD to rice mixture; toss to coat. Serve immediately or cover and refrigerate until ready to serve.

And use the ingredients you have on hand ...

What **veggies/fruit** are on hand?	And now for the **juice/peel**	Finish it off with a **seasoning**
peppers, green onions and 1 can (11 oz) mandarin-orange segments, drained	1/2 cup orange juice	dash ground ginger
mango and red onion	juice and grated peel of 1 lime	spoonful soy sauce
cooked asparagus spears and cherry tomatoes	juice and grated peel of 1 lemon	spoonful Dijon mustard and chopped fresh parsley
apples and celery	1 cup apple juice	dash curry powder

EASY ROASTED VEGETABLES

Just follow our 3 simple steps:
1 PLACE any combination of cut-up vegetables, such as potatoes, carrots, onions, Brussels sprouts or parsnips, in 9- x 13-inch baking dish.
2 POUR sun-dried tomato vinaigrette dressing over vegetables; toss to coat.
3 BAKE at 400°F for 1 hour or until vegetables are tender, stirring occasionally.

BROCCOLI-RICE CASSEROLE

Just follow our 3 simple steps:
1 COOK ½ cup chopped onion in 1 tablespoon butter or margarine in large skillet until tender, stirring frequently.
2 ADD 2 cups *each* cooked Minute White Rice and small broccoli florets, 1 can (10-¾ oz) condensed cream of mushroom soup and 1 cup Cheez Whiz; mix well. Spoon into 1-½-qt baking dish; sprinkle with ½ cup fresh bread cubes.
3 BAKE at 350°F for 30–35 minutes or until thoroughly heated.

AU GRATIN POTATOES

1 tub (8 oz) Philadelphia Cream Cheese Spread
2 tablespoons flour
2 cups milk
3 cups shredded sharp Cheddar cheese, divided
6 medium potatoes (about 2 lb) peeled, very thinly sliced
1 medium onion, thinly sliced

1 MIX cream cheese spread, flour and milk with wire whisk in medium saucepan until well blended. Cook on medium heat until cream cheese spread is melted and mixture is hot and bubbly, stirring frequently.
2 STIR in 2 cups of the Cheddar cheese; cook until completely melted, stirring frequently. Spread thin layer of cheese sauce on bottom of greased 9- x 13-inch baking dish. Layer potatoes, onion and cheese sauce alternately in baking dish. Season with salt and pepper; cover.
3 BAKE at 400°F for 1 hour or until potatoes are tender. Uncover; sprinkle with remaining 1 cup shredded Cheddar cheese. Bake an additional 5 minutes or until cheese is melted. *Serves 8.*

>> **TRY THIS, TOO**
Philadelphia Light Cream Cheese Spread makes a great substitute in these au gratin potatoes.

>> **FLAVORED MASHED POTATOES**
Stir ½ cup (half 8-oz tub) Philadelphia Chive & Onion or Light Roasted Garlic Cream Cheese Spread into 6 cups hot mashed potatoes until cream cheese spread is completely melted.

CORN PUDDING

>> TRY THIS, TOO
A delicious corn pudding can also be made by substituting 1 package (8-1/2 oz) corn-muffin mix for the baking mix, cornmeal and sugar.

1 can (15-1/4 oz) whole kernel corn, drained
1 can (14-3/4 oz) cream-style corn
1 cup sour cream
1 cup buttermilk baking mix
1/2 cup cornmeal
1/3 cup sugar
3 eggs, slightly beaten
1/4 cup margarine or butter, melted

1 MIX all ingredients until well blended.
2 POUR mixture into greased 9- x 13-inch baking dish.
3 BAKE at 375°F for 35–40 minutes, until edges are golden brown. *Serves 16.*

CLASSIC GREEN BEAN CASSEROLE

Just follow our 3 simple steps:
1 MIX 3 packages (9 oz *each*) French-cut green beans, thawed and drained, with 1 can (10-3/4 oz) condensed cream of mushroom soup, 1 cup Cheez Whiz and half of 1 can (2.8 oz) of French-fried onions in 1-1/2-qt baking dish.
2 BAKE at 350°F for 30 minutes.
3 TOP with remaining French-fried onions. Bake an additional 5 minutes.

PARMESAN GARLIC BREAD 4 WAYS

Just follow our 3 simple steps:
1 MIX 1 cup mayonnaise and ½ cup *each* shredded mozzarella cheese and grated Parmesan cheese.
2 ADD 1 garlic clove, minced; mix well. Spread evenly over toasted French baguette slices.
3 BAKE at 350°F for 5–7 minutes or until cheese mixture is melted. Serve immediately.

Parmesan Garlic Bread is also terrific in the following ways:

BACON-AND-ONION GARLIC BREAD
Prepare as directed, adding bacon bits and 2 green onions, sliced, to mayonnaise mixture and substituting toasted pumpernickel bread for toasted baguette slices.

BETTA BRUSCHETTA
Prepare as directed, adding chopped tomato and chopped red onion to mayonnaise mixture and substituting toasted Kaiser rolls, halved, for toasted baguette slices.

EXTRA-CHEESY GARLIC BREAD
Prepare as directed, substituting shredded Italian-style cheese for mozzarella cheese and toasted rye bread for toasted baguette slices.

5-INGREDIENT CHEDDAR BISCUITS

Just follow our 3 simple steps:

1 MIX 2 cups flour and 1 tablespoon baking powder. Cut in 1 tub (8 oz) cream cheese spread with 2 knives, a food processor or your hands to form a crumbly mixture.

2 STIR in ½ cup milk and a handful of shredded Cheddar cheese, if desired, stirring until dough holds together.

3 PAT dough ¾-inch thick on floured counter. Cut 10–12 biscuits with the top of a glass or with a cookie cutter. Place on baking sheet and bake at 425°F for 12–15 minutes.

At the heart of every pleasing meal, there's sure to be a main dish that performs on more than just one level. First, of course, it satisfies hunger. But a good main dish should also please the eye, tantalize with mouthwatering aromas and bring real pleasure to the taste buds. And did we forget to say that it should also be simple to make? Over the years, the Kraft Kitchens have learned a lot about

Main Dishes

what works best in kitchens just like yours. The great-tasting main dishes described in the pages that follow include many family favorites – frequently brought up-to-date with today's most popular ingredients and terrific time-saving techniques. Whether you're in the mood for an all-in-one skillet supper, a hearty casserole, the perfect freshly made sandwich, endlessly versatile chicken or even fish and chips, we're here with the perfect solution. You're about to discover those family classics all over again, and maybe even like them more than before.

Previous page: From a Kraft ad, 1985.

ITALIAN PASTA BAKE

1 lb lean ground beef or ground turkey
8 oz (about 3 cups) pasta, cooked and drained
1 jar (28 oz) spaghetti sauce
¾ cup Kraft 100% Grated Parmesan Cheese
2 cups shredded mozzarella cheese

1 BROWN meat in large skillet; drain. Stir in pasta, sauce and ½ cup of the Parmesan cheese.
2 SPOON into 9- x 13-inch baking dish; top with mozzarella cheese and remaining ¼ cup Parmesan cheese.
3 BAKE at 375°F for 20 minutes. *Serves 6.*

>> **VEGETABLE PASTA BAKE**
Prepare as directed, omitting ground meat and stirring in 1 package (16 oz) frozen mixed vegetables, thawed, with pasta.

EVERYDAY EASY LASAGNAS

Just follow our 3 simple steps:

1 BROWN **meat** and chopped **veggies** in a bit of oil in large skillet.

2 STIR in **sauce** and a couple handfuls of Kraft Shredded Mozzarella Cheese.

3 LAYER with oven-ready (no-boil) lasagna noodles in 9- x 13-inch baking dish; sprinkle with more cheese. Cover with foil and bake at 400°F for 30 minutes.

And use the ingredients you have on hand …

What **meat** do you feel like?	Add the **veggies**	And now for the **sauce**
1 lb boneless, skinless chicken strips	peppers	3 cups salsa and 1 cup water
1 lb ground beef	onions	3 cups spaghetti sauce and 1 cup water
2 handfuls sliced pepperoni	peppers	3 cups spaghetti sauce and 1 cup water
meatless	onions and mushrooms	2 cans (10-3/4 oz *each*) condensed cream of mushroom soup and 2 cans water

Everyday Easy Pepperoni Lasagna

VELVEETA ONE-PAN PLEASERS

Just follow our 3 simple steps:

1 BROWN **meat** (1 lb should do it for 4) in large skillet.

2 ADD **sauce** and 2 cups water. Bring to boil. Stir in 2 cups elbow macaroni or tiny shell pasta. Reduce heat to medium-low; cover with tight-fitting lid. Simmer 10-12 minutes or until pasta is tender.

3 ADD ¾ lb (12 oz) Velveeta, cut up, a few handfuls of **veggies** and dash of **seasonings**; cook until vegetables are heated. Let stand 5 minutes.

And use the ingredients you have on hand ...

>> TRY THIS, TOO
Substitute 1 package (14 oz) Velveeta Shells & Cheese for Velveeta and pasta. Prepare as directed, reducing water to 1-½ cups and increasing simmering time to 15 minutes.

What **meat** do you feel like?	What **sauce** do you have on hand?	Try these **veggies** and **seasonings**
boneless, skinless chicken breasts, cut up	1 can (10-3/4 oz) condensed cream of chicken soup	chopped broccoli, garlic powder
ground beef	1-1/2 cups salsa	corn, ground cumin
1 package (10 oz) smoked ham, chopped	1 can (10-3/4 oz) condensed cream of mushroom soup	mixed vegetable blend, Dijon mustard
1 can (6 oz) tuna, drained and flaked*	1 can (10-3/4 oz) condensed cream of celery soup	peas, Italian seasoning

*add with sauce and water

FAMILY-FAVORITE TUNA CASSEROLES

Just follow our 3 simple steps:

1 PLACE 2 cups **pasta** and 4 cups water in skillet; stir. Cook on high heat for 8-12 minutes or until pasta is tender, adding **veggies** (a few handfuls per person should do it) during final few minutes of pasta-cooking time.
2 REDUCE heat to medium. Stir in 1 can (10 -¾ oz) condensed cream of mushroom soup, 1 can (6 oz) tuna, drained and flaked, and a few handfuls of **Kraft Shredded Cheese**.
3 TOP with a few more handfuls of cheese; cover. Cook an additional 2 minutes or until cheese is melted.

And use the ingredients you have on hand …

What **pasta** do you feel like?	Try these **veggies**	Add this **Kraft Shredded Cheese**
elbow macaroni	peas, sliced celery	Cheddar
rotini	broccoli florets	Italian Style
fusilli	peas, sliced carrots	Cheddar
small shells	corn	Mexican Style

Tuna Casserole with Broccoli

15-MINUTE RICE DINNERS

Just follow our 3 simple steps:

1 COOK **meat** in a little oil in large covered skillet for about 10 minutes. Additional time will be required for chicken and less time for ham.

2 ADD **liquid** and 2 cups uncooked Minute White Rice (enough to serve 4). Bring to boil.

3 STIR in **add-ins**; cover. Let stand 5 minutes before serving.

And use the ingredients you have on hand ...

>> SHARING OUR EXPERIENCES
Whenever I have leftover meat, rice or vegetables, I make a great lunch the next day. Fill large warmed flour tortillas with a few spoonfuls of warmed-up leftovers, roll and serve.
—Michele, Kraft Kitchens

What **meat** do you feel like?	Choose a **liquid** for sauce and flavor	Finish it with **add-ins**
4 boneless, skinless chicken breast halves	1 can (10-3/4 oz) condensed cream of chicken soup and 1 can water	salt and pepper
1 lb ground beef	1 cup *each* salsa and water	shredded Cheddar cheese, corn
2 cups chopped cooked ham	1 can (14 oz) pineapple tidbits and 1 can water	chopped peppers
6 boneless chicken thighs	1 can (10-3/4 oz) condensed cream of chicken soup and 1 can water	1 package (16 oz) frozen stir-fry veggies (thawed), a few spoonfuls soy sauce

3-CHEESE BAKED MACARONI & CHEESE

Just follow our 3 simple steps:

1 PREPARE 1 package (14 oz) Kraft Deluxe Macaroni & Cheese Dinner as directed on package. Stir in ½ cup shredded mozzarella cheese and 1 cup milk.

2 SPOON into greased 1-½-qt casserole. Sprinkle with 1 cup shredded Cheddar cheese.

3 BAKE at 375°F for 20 minutes or until thoroughly heated.

3-Cheese Baked Macaroni & Cheese is also terrific in the following ways:

HAM-AND-BROCCOLI BAKED MACARONI & CHEESE

Prepare macaroni & cheese mixture as directed, stirring in a couple hand-fuls *each* chopped ham and frozen chopped broccoli, thawed, and a spoon-ful Dijon mustard with mozzarella cheese.

TACO MAC SQUARES

Prepare macaroni & cheese mixture as directed. Spoon into 8-inch square baking dish. Cook and season 1 lb lean ground beef with 1 package (1-¼ oz) taco-seasoning mix as directed on package. Spoon over mixture; sprinkle with Cheddar cheese. Bake as directed.

>> **KRAFT KITCHENS TIP** To make this casserole extra special, sprinkle ½ cup crushed buttery crackers over casserole before baking.

SIMPLE SPAGHETTI AND MEATBALLS

Just follow our 2 simple steps:

1 COOK spaghetti as directed on package; drain. Meanwhile, mix 1 jar (26 oz) spaghetti sauce and prepared Master Meatballs (see below; use about 4–5 meatballs per serving) in large skillet; cook on medium-high until thoroughly heated, stirring occasionally.

2 PLACE cooked spaghetti in serving bowl; top with sauce mixture. Sprinkle with grated Parmesan cheese.

MASTER MEATBALLS

Just follow our 3 simple steps:

1 MIX 1 lb extra-lean ground beef with ½ cup *each* dry bread crumbs and barbecue sauce, 1 egg and a few spoonfuls of grated Parmesan cheese until well blended.

2 ROLL into 1-inch balls; place in 15- x 10- x 1-inch baking pan.

3 BAKE at 400°F for 20 minutes, until meatballs are cooked through.

>> **KRAFT KITCHENS TIP**
You can freeze cooked meatballs with prepared sauce in a sealable plastic freezer bag.

15-MINUTE STROGANOFFS

>> **KRAFT KITCHENS TIP**
Reduced-fat sour cream and
light cream cheese spread
make great substitutes in
this dish.

Just follow our 3 simple steps:

1 COOK **meat** (1 lb should do it for 4) and 1 onion, chopped, in a large
skillet with a little oil. Add **veggies/fruit** (a handful per person).

2 ADD 2 cups **broth** and 2 cups uncooked wide egg noodles. Bring to boil;
cover. Reduce heat and simmer 10 minutes. Remove from heat.

3 STIR in 1 cup sour cream or 1 tub (8 oz) cream cheese spread; cover.
Let stand 5 minutes.

And use the ingredients you have on hand …

What **meat** do you feel like?	What **veggies/fruit** do you have on hand?	Add the **broth**
boneless, skinless chicken, sliced	pepper strips	chicken
sirloin steak, sliced	sliced mushrooms	beef
pork tenderloin, sliced	sliced apples	chicken
meatless	sliced mushrooms, frozen mixed veggies	vegetable

SPEEDY À LA KING SUPPERS

Just follow our 2 simple steps:

1 PLACE 1 tub (8 oz) cream cheese spread, ½ cup milk, **meat** and a couple handfuls of chopped **veggies** in saucepan; cook on medium for 8-10 minutes or until heated through, stirring occasionally.

2 SERVE over your favorite **base**.

And use the ingredients you have on hand …

What **meat** do you feel like?	Now for the **veggies**	Serve over this **base**
2 cups chopped cooked chicken	chopped peppers, frozen peas (thawed)	frozen puff pastry shells, baked
1 can (6 oz) tuna, drained and flaked	small broccoli florets, chopped onion	cooked noodles
2 cups chopped ham	frozen mixed vegetables (thawed)	toast
meatless	sliced mushrooms and zucchini, chopped pepper	cooked rice

STOVE TOP ONE-DISH CHICKEN BAKE

>> TRY THIS, TOO
Top chicken with 2 cups frozen mixed vegetables, thawed, before covering with soup mixture.

You can also use reduced-fat sour cream in this dish.

1 package (6 oz) or 2 packages (120 g *each*) Stove Top Stuffing Mix for Chicken
¼ cup butter or margarine, cut up
1-½ cups hot water
4 boneless, skinless chicken breast halves (about 1-¼ lb)
1 can (10-¾ oz) condensed cream of mushroom soup
⅓ cup sour cream or milk

1 MIX contents of stuffing mix pouch, butter and hot water; set aside. Place chicken in 9- x 13-inch baking dish.
2 MIX soup and sour cream; pour over chicken. Top with stuffing mixture.
3 BAKE at 375°F for 35 minutes or until chicken is cooked through.
Serves 4.

20-MINUTE STUFFING SKILLET

Just follow our 3 simple steps:

1 MELT a little butter or margarine in large nonstick skillet on medium–high heat. Add **meat** (1 lb should do it for 4); cover. Cook 4 minutes on each side or until cooked through. Remove from skillet.

2 ADD 1-⅔ cups water and a few handfuls **veggies**; bring to boil. Stir in 1 package (6 oz) or 2 packages (120 g *each*) Stove Top Stuffing Mix, any flavor, just to moisten. Return meat to skillet. Season with salt and pepper to taste.

3 SPOON **sauce** over meat; sprinkle with **Kraft Shredded Cheese**; cover. Cook on low heat 5 minutes.

And use the ingredients you have on hand …

What **meat** do you feel like?	What **veggies** do you have on hand?	Try these **sauces** and **Kraft Shredded Cheeses**
boneless, skinless chicken breasts	canned or thawed frozen mixed vegetables	prepared gravy, Cheddar
boneless, skinless chicken breasts	chopped peppers	salsa, Mexican Style cheese
boneless pork chops	corn	barbecue sauce, Cheddar
meatless (use 6-8 oz Portobello mushroom slices*)	chopped zucchini	mushroom gravy, Swiss

cooked in butter 2 minutes, stirring occasionally

30-MINUTE POT PIES

Just follow our 3 simple steps:

1 MIX 2 cups frozen mixed vegetables, cubed cooked **meat** (leftovers are great here) and **sauce** ingredients in 9-inch pie plate or 2-qt baking dish.

2 PREPARE **topping**; arrange over meat mixture.

3 BAKE at 350°F for 30 minutes.

And use the ingredients you have on hand …

What **meat** do you feel like?	What **sauce** do you like?	Now for the **topping**
chicken	1 can (10-3/4 oz) condensed cream of chicken soup and 1/4 cup milk	1 frozen pie shell, inverted over filling
ham	Cheez Whiz (about 1 cup)	i can (10 oz) refrigerated biscuits, cut into quarters
turkey	1 can (10-3/4 oz) condensed cream of mushroom soup and 1/4 cup milk	1 package (6 oz) stuffing mix, any flavor
meatless (use cubed tofu)	1 can (10-3/4 oz) condensed cream of broccoli soup and 1/4 cup milk	frozen puff pastry, thawed, rolled and cut to fit top of baking dish

30-Minute Chicken Pot Pie

EASY PLEASING MEATLOAF

Just follow our 3 simple steps:

1 MIX 2 lb lean ground beef or ground turkey, 1 cup water, 1 package (6 oz) or 2 packages (120 g *each*) Stove Top Stuffing Mix, any variety, 2 eggs, beaten, and ¼ cup barbecue sauce.

2 SHAPE meat mixture into oval loaf and place in 9-x 13-inch baking dish; top with additional ¼ cup barbecue sauce.

3 BAKE at 375°F for 1 hour or until center is no longer pink.

>> **SHARING OUR EXPERIENCES**

The kids love it when I make meatloaf in muffin cups. Prepare as directed, then press the meat mixture into 12 muffin cups. Bake at 375°F for 30 minutes or until the centers are no longer pink.

—Maxine, Kraft Kitchens

SIMPLE SHEPHERDS' PIES

>> TRY THIS, TOO
Try homemade biscuit
topping with the steak pie,
mashed sweet potatoes
with the ham version
or cooked rice with the
ground beef pie.

Just follow our 3 simple steps:

1 BROWN **meat** (1 lb should do it for 4) in ovenproof skillet; drain fat.

2 ADD a few handfuls of sliced **veggies** and 1 cup **Kraft Dressing** to meat mixture; cook and stir until veggies are tender. Top generously with homemade mashed potatoes (leftovers work well) or prepared instant mashed potatoes.

3 BROIL 5 minutes or until mashed potatoes are lightly brown on surface.

And use the ingredients you have on hand …

What **meat** do you feel like?	Now for the **veggies**	And try this **Kraft Dressing**
ground beef	sliced carrots, corn	Classic Caesar
chopped ham	green beans, sliced mushrooms	Ranch
sliced sirloin	broccoli florets, sliced carrots	Catalina
meatless	cauliflower florets, chopped peppers and sliced zucchini	Peppercorn Ranch

Shepherds' Pie with Ground Beef

EASY SKILLET CHICKEN

Just follow our 3 simple steps:

1 MOISTEN 6 boneless, skinless chicken breast halves with water; shake off excess.

2 SHAKE chicken, 1 or 2 pieces at a time, in Shake'N Bake Original Chicken Seasoned Coating Mix. Discard any remaining coating mix and bag.

3 HEAT a spoonful of oil in large skillet on medium heat. Add chicken. Cook 7 minutes; turn. Cook an additional 7-8 minutes or until chicken is cooked through.

Easy Skillet Chicken is also terrific in the following ways:

EASY SKILLET CHICKEN WITH LEMON SAUCE

Prepare as directed. Mix equal parts sour cream and mayonnaise. Stir in a few spoonfuls lemon juice. Serve over chicken.

EASY SKILLET MEXICAN CHICKEN

Prepare as directed. Top chicken with 1 cup salsa and 1 cup Mexican-style shredded cheese; cover. Cook an additional 2-4 minutes or until cheese is melted.

>> KRAFT KITCHENS TIP
Chicken pieces can be coated and stored in the refrigerator until ready to cook, up to 1 day in advance.

You can also use reduced-fat sour cream and light mayonnaise in the Lemon Sauce version of this dish.

BAKED CATALINA CHICKEN

>> KRAFT KITCHENS TIPS
Catalina Chicken will likely
make enough for 2 meals –
share half your cooking with
a friend who has recently
had a baby or is just home
after a hospital stay.

Catalina Chicken reheats
well in a microwave oven or
in a conventional oven.

Just follow our 3 simple steps:
1 PLACE 5-6 lb chicken pieces in 2 (9- x 13-inch) baking pans.
2 MIX 1 can (16 oz) whole-berry cranberry sauce, 1 bottle (8 oz) Kraft
Catalina Dressing and 1 package (2 oz) dry onion-soup mix; pour evenly
over chicken.
3 BAKE at 350°F for 1 hour or until cooked through.

OVEN-BAKED FISH AND CHIPS

Just follow our 3 simple steps:
1 SHAKE 1 block frozen fish in original or extra-crispy seasoned coating mix.
2 PLACE on baking sheet with 1 package (24 oz) frozen potato wedges.
3 BAKE at 450°F for 20 minutes or until fish flakes easily and potatoes are
golden brown.

3-STEP CHILI DINNERS

Just follow our 3 simple steps:

1 COOK ground **meat** (1 lb should do it for 4) and a few handfuls of sliced **veggies** in ¼ cup Italian dressing until meat is cooked and veggies are tender.
2 ADD 1 can (19 oz) *each* undrained diced tomatoes and kidney beans and a few dashes *each* garlic powder and chili powder. Bring to boil. Reduce heat to medium–low; simmer 10 minutes.
3 STIR in a few handfuls of **Kraft Shredded Cheese**; cook until melted. Top with additional cheese just before serving.

And use the ingredients you have on hand …

» TRY THIS, TOO
3-Step Chili tastes great with our 5-Ingredient Cheddar Biscuits (page 53).

What ground **meat** do you feel like?	What **veggies** do you have on hand?	Add this **Kraft Shredded Cheese**
chicken	sliced mushrooms and carrots	Italian Style
beef	chopped onions and peppers	Mexican Style
pork	sliced celery and zucchini	Cheddar
meatless (use 1 cup rice)	corn, sliced celery and chopped onion	Mexican Style

SLOW-COOKER BEEF STEWS

>> KRAFT KITCHENS TIPS

The ingredients for this recipe can be prepared the night before. Cover and refrigerate until ready to use. In the morning, transfer ingredients to slow-cooker container and cook as directed.

Cut veggies into same-sized pieces so they cook evenly. If using frozen veggies, add just 30 minutes before serving.

Just follow our 3 simple steps:

1 ADD cubes of stewing beef (2 lb should do it for 4) and a chopped onion to slow-cooker container.

2 ADD **veggies** (a couple handfuls of *each*) and **sauce** ingredients (1 cup of *each*) to meat mixture; cover with lid.

3 COOK on LOW setting for 6-7 hours or until meat is cooked through and veggies are tender. Finish with one of our **serving suggestions**.

And use the ingredients you have on hand …

Try these **veggies**	Add these **sauce** ingredients	And choose a **serving suggestion**
sliced mushrooms, cut green beans	regular barbecue sauce, beef broth	stir in spoonful of sour cream, serve over noodles
sliced celery and mushrooms	barbecue sauce with onion bits, dry red wine	serve over rice
sliced squash, chopped peppers	spicy barbecue sauce, beef broth	stir in corn, top with cheese and tortilla chips
sliced carrots and celery	sweet-and-sour sauce, chicken broth	serve with rice, top with chow mein noodles

Beef Stew with Carrots and Celery

SLOW-SIMMERED SLOPPY JOES

Just follow our 3 simple steps:

1 BROWN lean ground beef or ground turkey (2 lb should do for 8) in large skillet; drain.

2 MIX meat, **sauce** and ½ cup water in slow-cooker; cover with lid.

3 COOK on LOW setting for 4-6 hours. Fill split hamburger buns with meat mixture and **Kraft Cheese**.

And use the ingredients you have on hand …

Try one of these **sauces**	Try this **Kraft Cheese**
1 bottle (18 oz) barbecue sauce	Cheez Whiz
1 jar (16 oz) salsa and 1 package (1-1/4 oz) taco-seasoning mix	Mexican Style Shredded
1 jar (14 oz) spaghetti sauce	Shredded Mozzarella
1 bottle (14 oz) ketchup and 1 tablespoon mustard	Kraft Singles

ALL-AMERICAN DELUXE CHEESEBURGERS

Just follow our 3 simple steps:

1 MIX 1 lb ground beef with **seasoning/sauce** and shape into 4 patties.

2 COOK patties in skillet on medium heat, 4-6 minutes on each side or until cooked through. Top each patty with Kraft Singles; cover. Continue to heat until Singles are melted.

3 GARNISH with lettuce, tomato and your favorite **toppings**. Serve on toasted Kaiser or hamburger rolls.

And use the ingredients you have on hand …

Which **seasoning/sauce** do you feel like?	And now for the **toppings**
1 package (1-1/4 oz) taco-seasoning mix	salsa
2 tablespoons barbecue sauce	barbecue sauce and crisply cooked bacon
2 tablespoons pizza sauce	pizza sauce and sliced pepperoni
2 tablespoons ketchup	ketchup, mustard and pickles

All-American Deluxe Bacon Cheeseburger

EASY DINNER MELTS

Just follow our 3 simple steps:

1 MIX chopped **meat** with a couple spoonfuls of Miracle Whip, a few handfuls of **Kraft Shredded Cheese** and **add-ins**. Spread on favorite bread (such as English muffins, crusty rolls, bagels, pizza crust).

2 BAKE at 400°F for 20 minutes.

3 ADD extra toppings (see our kitchen tip) and serve.

And use the ingredients you have on hand …

>> KRAFT KITCHENS TIP
Dill pickles, sliced avocado, lettuce and tomato all make great toppings to these Easy Dinner Melts.

What **meat** do you feel like?	Add some **Kraft Shredded Cheese**	And now for the **add-ins**
cooked chicken	Mexican Style	sliced green onion and salsa
cooked turkey	Mozzarella	chopped green onion
cooked ham	Italian Style	chopped pickle
meatless (use hard-cooked egg)	Cheddar	pinch of dry mustard

15-MINUTE SOFT TACOS

Just follow our 3 simple steps:

1 BROWN lean ground **meat** (1 lb should do it for 4) in large nonstick skillet.

2 STIR IN 2 cups *each* water and Minute White Rice and 1 package (1–¼ oz) taco-seasoning mix. Bring to boil.

3 SPRINKLE with Mexican-style shredded cheese, let stand 5 minutes. Spoon meat mixture evenly onto flour tortillas, then add sliced **veggies** and **topping**.

And use the ingredients you have on hand …

What ground **meat** do you feel like?	What **veggies** do you have on hand?	And now for the **topping**
chicken	tomatoes, peppers	salsa
beef	peppers, corn	guacamole
pork	tomatoes, onions	salsa
meatless (use 1 can/19 oz kidney beans, drained)	tomatoes, green onions	sour cream

CHEESY QUESADILLAS

Just follow our 2 simple steps:

1 PLACE 1 tortilla on microwavable plate. Place **Kraft Cheese** on half of tortilla, then add a small handful *each* of chopped **meat** and **veggies**. Fold tortilla in half to cover cheese. Cover.

2 MICROWAVE on HIGH 25-40 seconds or until cheese begins to melt. Let stand, covered, 1 minute or until cool enough to eat. Serve with salsa.

And use the ingredients you have on hand …

What **Kraft Cheese** do you feel like?	Add the **meat**	And now for the **veggies**
Cheez Whiz	cooked bacon	onions, peppers
Kraft Singles	cooked chicken	tomatoes, avocados
Shredded Cheddar	pepperoni	black olives, peppers
Mexican Style Shredded	meatless	black beans, corn, green onions

Cheesy Quesadillas with Tomato and Avocado

SIMPLE SANDWICH FILLINGS

Just follow our 2 simple steps:

1 MIX ½ cup Miracle Whip with chopped cooked **meat** (½ lb should do it for 4 sandwiches), 2 stalks celery, chopped, and 2 green onions, chopped.

2 ADD a handful of chopped **add-ins** and a spoonful of **flavoring**. Use as sandwich filling or serve with crackers.

And use the ingredients you have on hand …

What **meat** do you feel like?	What **add-ins** do you have on hand?	And now for the **flavoring**
chicken	toasted almonds	sweetened dried cranberries
tuna	green apple, raisins	curry powder
salmon	teriyaki sauce	ground ginger
meatless (use 4 hard-cooked eggs)	tomatoes	ground cumin

Nearly everyone has a favorite sweet, and some of us have a few more than just one or two. In this handy easy-to-follow cookbook, we've collected a wide range of old favorites to satisfy almost every personal preference. Luscious cheesecakes, chocolate goodies in many guises, a whole range of Jell-O treats, puddings, cakes, squares and more can be found in the pages just ahead.

Desserts

Desserts don't have to be difficult - now you can enjoy time with your guests, too. Savor every bite: A little bit can go a long way to satisfy your sweet tooth. If a batch of child-pleasing cookies or a layer cake guaranteed to make you feel nostalgic is on the agenda, all you have to do is read on. If butter tarts, an apple pie or moist muffins are what you're after, you need look no further. Just read on, and satisfy that craving for something sweet right now. Before you know it, those goodies will be ready to enjoy. And don't forget the coffee!

CLASSIC COOKIE CRUSTS

Just follow our 2 simple steps:

1 MIX **cookies**, finely crushed (about 1-¼ cups crumbs), ¼ cup sugar and ⅓ cup melted butter or margarine in small bowl; press mixture firmly onto bottom and up inside of 9-inch pie plate.

2 BAKE at 375°F for 8-10 minutes. Cool completely. Use as a base with any of the suggested **fillings**.

And use the ingredients you have on hand …

>> KRAFT KITCHENS TIP
To crush cookies, place in large sealable plastic bag, squeeze out air and seal. Run rolling pin back and forth over surface. Or crush in food processor or blender.

What **cookie** do you feel like?	How many cookies do you need?	Great **filling** ideas
chocolate sandwich	15	chocolate-chip ice cream
vanilla wafer	35	butter-pecan ice cream
graham cracker	14-16 squares	vanilla pudding
gingersnap	20	butterscotch pudding

CHEDDAR-CRUST APPLE PIE

>> **KRAFT KITCHENS TIP**
Rolling the crust between
2 sheets of waxed paper
prevents sticking and makes
it easier to transfer the
crust to the pie plate.

1-½ cups flour
½ cup shortening
1-½ cups shredded Cheddar cheese
4 to 6 tablespoons water
½ cup sugar
2 tablespoons flour
½ teaspoon ground cinnamon
6 cups sliced peeled apples
2 tablespoons butter or margarine

1 MIX 1-½ cups flour and shortening with pastry blender or 2 forks until mixture resembles coarse crumbs. Stir in cheese.

2 ADD water; mix lightly with fork. Form into ball. Divide dough in half. Roll one half to 11-inch circle on lightly floured surface. Place in 9-inch pie plate.

3 MIX sugar, 2 tablespoons flour and cinnamon. Toss with apples; place in pie shell. Dot with butter. Roll out remaining pastry to 11-inch circle; place over apple filling. Seal and flute edge. Cut several slits to permit steam to escape. Bake at 425°F for 35 minutes or until golden brown. *Serves 8.*

RITZ MOCK APPLE PIE

Pastry for double-crust pie

36 Ritz Crackers, coarsely broken (about 1-3/4 cups crumbs)

2 cups sugar

1-3/4 cups water

2 teaspoons cream of tartar

2 tablespoons lemon juice

Grated peel of 1 lemon

2 tablespoons butter or margarine

Few dashes ground cinnamon

1 PLACE 1 pie crust in 9-inch pie plate. Place cracker crumbs in crust.

2 HEAT sugar, water and cream of tartar to boil in saucepan on high heat. Reduce heat to medium–low; simmer 15 minutes. Add lemon juice and peel; cool. Pour syrup over cracker crumbs. Dot with butter; sprinkle with cinnamon. Place remaining crust over pie. Slit top and trim edges. Pinch edges with fork to seal.

3 BAKE at 425°F for 30–35 minutes or until crust is golden. Cool completely. *Serves 10.*

>> **INSIDE A CLASSIC**
Mock Apple Pie's popularity soared during World War II, when fresh apples were hard to come by.

ANY FRUIT PIES

>> TRY THIS, TOO
Any Fruit Pies can also be made with a ready-made cookie crust.

Just follow our 3 simple steps:

1 MIX 1–½ cups finely crushed **cookie crumbs** and ⅓ cup melted butter or margarine. Press onto bottom and up inside of 9-inch pie plate.
2 DISSOLVE 1 package (4-serving size) **gelatin** in ¾ cup boiling water. Add 2 cups ice cubes. Stir until gelatin is thickened; remove any unmelted ice.
3 ADD 2 cups thawed whipped topping and a cupful of fresh or canned **fruit**, drained; stir gently. Refrigerate 10 minutes or until filling is thick. Spoon into prepared crust. Refrigerate until filling is set.

And use the ingredients you have on hand …

What **cookie crumbs** do you feel like?	Try this flavor of **gelatin**	And now for the **fruit**
chocolate sandwich	cherry	pitted sweet cherries
graham cracker	strawberry	strawberries, raspberries and/or blueberries
graham cracker	lemon	sliced peeled apricots
vanilla wafer	orange	sliced peeled peaches

Any Fruit Peach Pie and Mixed Berry Pie

CREAMY DOUBLE-LAYER PIE

Just follow our 3 simple steps:

1 POUR 1-¾ cups cold milk into large bowl. Add 2 packages (4-serving size *each*) **Jell-O Instant Pudding & Pie Filling**. Beat 2 minutes with wire whisk or until well blended. Gently stir in 2 cups thawed whipped topping.

2 SPOON into 9-inch prepared **crumb crust** (page 107) .

3 SPREAD additional whipped topping over pudding. Refrigerate 3 hours or until set. Add finishing **topping**.

And use the ingredients you have on hand …

>> **KRAFT KITCHENS TIP**
Make this delicious dessert in even less time by using a ready-made crumb crust.

What flavor **Jell-O Instant Pudding & Pie Filling?**	Pour into this **crumb crust**	Finish with this **topping**
chocolate	chocolate	chopped chocolate wafers
vanilla	gingersnap	sliced strawberries
lemon	vanilla wafer	fresh blueberries
butterscotch	graham cracker	caramel sauce

CLASSIC BUTTER TARTS

>> **CHOCOLATE BUTTER TARTS**

Omit raisins. Chop 3 squares of bittersweet chocolate into 12 pieces. Place 1 chunk on bottom of each tart shell before filling and baking. Drizzle baked tarts with more melted chocolate.

Just follow our 3 simple steps:

1 MIX ¾ cup packed brown sugar, ¼ cup corn syrup, 1 egg, 2 tablespoons softened butter or margarine, 1 teaspoon vanilla and a handful of raisins.
2 SPOON into 12 unbaked medium tart shells, filling ¾ full.
3 BAKE at 450°F for 12-14 minutes or until filling is puffed and bubbly and pastry is light golden. Let cool on racks.

>> **KRAFT KITCHENS TIP** Make your own tart shells: Cut 12 (4-inch) circles from 1 package (15 oz) refrigerated pie crust (2 crusts; 6 circles per crust). Line 12 muffin tins with pie-crust circles, pressing the crust onto the bottom and inside of each cup and forming lip at the top of each. Fill and bake as directed. Run a sharp knife around edges of each tin to loosen tarts, if necessary.

HEAVENLY CHOCOLATE CAKE

CAKE

1 package (2-layer size) chocolate cake mix (not pudding-in-the-mix variety)

½ cup unsweetened cocoa

3 eggs

1-⅓ cups water

1 cup Miracle Whip

FROSTING

1 package (8 oz) cream cheese, softened

2 tablespoons milk

1 teaspoon vanilla

5 cups sifted powdered sugar

½ cup unsweetened cocoa

>> **KRAFT KITCHEN TIP**
Make it a single-layer cake: Use greased and floured 9- x 13-inch baking pan. Bake at 350°F for 35-40 minutes or until toothpick inserted in center comes out clean. Cool completely. Spread frosting over cake.

For the cake:

1 STIR cake mix and ½ cup cocoa in a bowl. Add eggs, water and Miracle Whip; beat on low speed 30 seconds, scraping bowl often. Beat on medium speed 2 minutes. Grease and flour 2 (9-inch) round cake pans. Line bottoms of pans with waxed paper. Pour batter into pans.

2 BAKE at 350°F for 30-35 minutes or until toothpick inserted in center comes out clean. Cool 10 minutes; remove from pans and immediately peel off waxed paper. Cool completely on wire racks.

For the frosting:

3 BEAT cream cheese, milk and vanilla until well blended. Mix sugar and remaining ½ cup cocoa. Gradually add to cream cheese mixture, beating well after each addition. Fill and frost cake layers. *Serves 16.*

RUM-NUT PUDDING CAKE

>> **KRAFT KITCHENS TIP**
To make warm syrup for
Rum-Nut Pudding Cake,
mix 1 cup sugar, ½ cup
butter or margarine and
¼ cup water in saucepan.
Cook, stirring frequently,
until mixture comes
to a boil; boil 5 minutes.
Slowly add ½ cup rum.
Pour over cake.

Just follow our 3 simple steps:

1 SPRINKLE a handful of chopped pecans onto bottom of greased fluted tube pan.

2 BEAT 1 package (4-serving size) vanilla instant pudding-and-pie filling, 1 package (2-layer size) white cake mix, 4 eggs and ½ cup *each* water, oil and rum in large bowl with electric mixer.

3 POUR into pan and bake at 350°F for about 50 minutes. Cool slightly. Remove cake from pan, prick with wooden pick or fork. Pour warm syrup over cake.

EASY FROSTED CARROT CAKE

Just follow our 3 simple steps:

1 PREPARE 1 package (2-layer size) carrot cake mix as directed on package for 9- x 13-inch baking pan. Cool completely.

2 BEAT 1 package (8 oz) cream cheese, softened, ⅓ cup sugar and ¼ cup milk until well blended. Gently stir in 4 cups thawed whipped topping. Spread over top of cake.

3 REFRIGERATE until ready to serve. Garnish as desired.

>> **TRY THIS, TOO** You can substitute spice cake mix for carrot cake mix and stir in 4 grated carrots to make an equally pleasing spicy variation.

JELL-O POKE CAKE

Just follow our 3 simple steps:

1 PLACE 2 baked 9-inch round white cake layers, cooled, top sides up, in 2 clean 9-inch round cake pans. Pierce cake with fork at ½-inch intervals.

2 STIR 1 cup boiling water into 1 package (4-serving size) any flavor Jell-O Gelatin. Repeat with 1 cup boiling water and different flavor Jell-O Gelatin in separate bowl. Carefully pour 1 flavor of gelatin over each cake layer.

3 REFRIGERATE 3 hours. Dip 1 cake pan in warm water 10 seconds. Unmold onto serving plate. Frost top with about 1 cup whipped topping. Unmold second cake layer; carefully place on first layer. Frost top and sides of cake with additional whipped topping.

JELL-O PUDDING POKE CAKE

Just follow our 3 simple steps:

1 PREPARE and bake 1 package (2-layer size) any flavor cake mix as directed on package for 9- x 13-inch baking pan. Remove from oven. Immediately poke large holes down through cake to pan with round handle of a wooden spoon, at 1-inch intervals.

2 POUR 4 cups cold milk into large bowl. Add 2 packages (4-serving size *each*) any flavor Jell-O Instant Pudding & Pie Filling. Beat 2 minutes. Immediately pour half the pudding evenly over warm cake and into holes. Let remaining pudding mixture stand to thicken slightly.

3 FROST cake with remaining pudding.

>> KRAFT KITCHENS TIPS
Refrigerate cake at least 1 hour or until ready to serve. Store leftovers in refrigerator.

Dress up this dessert by sprinkling multi-colored sprinkles, chocolate shavings, chopped nuts or toasted coconut over finished cake.

MIDNIGHT BLISS CAKE

>> **KRAFT KITCHENS TIP**
To remove cake from pan,
loosen cake from side of pan
with small knife or spatula.
Invert cake onto rack and
gently remove cake.

1 package (2-layer size) chocolate cake mix
1 package (4-serving size) chocolate instant pudding-and-pie filling
½ cup French vanilla instant-coffee drink mix
4 eggs
1 cup sour cream
½ cup *each* oil and water
1 package (8 oz) Baker's Semi-Sweet Baking Chocolate, chopped

1 PLACE cake mix, pudding mix, coffee mix, eggs, sour cream, oil and water
in large bowl. Beat with electric mixer on low speed just until moistened.
Beat on medium speed 2 minutes or until well blended. Stir in chocolate.
2 POUR into lightly greased and floured 12-cup fluted tube pan or
10-inch tube pan.
3 BAKE at 350°F for 50-60 minutes or until toothpick inserted near
center comes out clean. Cool 10 minutes on wire rack. Remove from pan.
Sprinkle with powdered sugar, if desired. *Serves 12.*

Midnight Bliss Cake; in back, Rum-Nut Pudding Cake and Heavenly Chocolate Cake

RED VELVET CAKE

CAKE
1 package (2-layer size) white cake mix
2 squares unsweetened baking chocolate, melted
2 tablespoons red food coloring
FROSTING
1 package (8 oz) cream cheese, softened
½ cup butter or margarine, softened
1 package (16 oz) powdered sugar

For the cake:
1 PREPARE and bake cake mix as directed on package for 9- x 13-inch pan, adding chocolate and food coloring (along with amounts of water, eggs and oil specified on the package); cool completely.
For the frosting:
2 BEAT cream cheese and butter until well blended, to prepare frosting. Gradually add sugar, beating until smooth. Spread on cake. *Serves 12.*

>> TRY THIS, TOO Sprinkle with ½ cup chopped pecans as a special treat.

>> **INSIDE A CLASSIC**
The Red Velvet Cake is especially popular in the southern United States, even though it originated at the Waldorf-Astoria Hotel in New York City.

PHILADELPHIA 3-STEP CHEESECAKE

▶▶ KRAFT KITCHENS TIP
To make a party-sized cheesecake: Mix 2 cups crushed graham crackers, ⅓ cup sugar and 6 tablespoons melted butter or margarine. Press on bottom of 9- x 13-inch glass baking dish. Double the recipe for cheesecake filling, pour over crust and bake at 325°F for 40–50 minutes or until center is almost set. Cool and serve as directed.

Just follow our 3 simple steps:

1 BEAT 2 packages (8 oz *each*) Philadelphia Cream Cheese, softened; ½ cup sugar, ½ teaspoon vanilla and **add-ins** until smooth. Add 2 eggs, 1 at a time; mix until just blended.

2 POUR into ready-to-use graham cracker crust. Sprinkle with **toppers**.

3 BAKE at 325°F for 40–45 minutes or until center is almost set. Cool. Refrigerate 3 hours or overnight. Serve with a dollop of whipped topping.

And use the ingredients you have on hand …

Choose these **add-ins**	And now for the **toppers**
1/2 teaspoon grated lemon peel	sliced assorted fresh fruit, drizzled with warm apple jelly or strawberry jam*
4 squares semisweet chocolate, melted	miniature marshmallows, semisweet chocolate chunks and chopped peanuts
1/2 cup canned pumpkin, dash *each* ground cinnamon ground cloves and nutmeg	chocolate-covered English toffee bars, coarsely chopped
a few handfuls mini chocolate-sandwich cookies	semisweet chocolate, melted, with a little whipping cream*

*top after baking

Fruit-Topped Lemon 3-Step Cheesecake

CLASSIC NEW YORK CHEESECAKE

CRUST
1 cup graham cracker crumbs
3 tablespoons sugar
3 tablespoons butter or margarine, melted
FILLING
5 packages (8 oz *each*) Philadelphia Cream Cheese, softened
1 cup sugar
3 tablespoons flour
1 tablespoon vanilla
1 cup sour cream
3 eggs
1 can (21 oz) cherry pie filling

For the crust:
1 MIX graham cracker crumbs, 3 tablespoons sugar and butter. Press firmly onto bottom of 9-inch springform pan. Bake at 350°F for 10 minutes.
For the filling:
2 BEAT cream cheese, 1 cup sugar, flour and vanilla until well blended. Blend in sour cream. Add eggs, 1 at a time, mixing on low speed after each addition just until blended. Pour over crust.
3 BAKE at 350°F for 1 hour or until center is almost set. Run knife around rim of pan to loosen cake; cool before removing rim of pan. Refrigerate 4 hours or overnight. Top with pie filling just before serving. *Serves 16.*

>> **INSIDE A CLASSIC**
Philadelphia Brand cream cheese was introduced in 1880, named as a tribute to Philadelphia, which was considered a home to fine food.

STRIPED DELIGHT

½ cup butter or margarine, melted
1 cup flour
2 tablespoons sugar
Chopped nuts
1 package (8 oz) cream cheese, softened
1 cup powdered sugar
2 cups thawed Cool Whip Whipped Topping
1 package (4-serving size) chocolate instant pudding-and-pie filling
1 package (4-serving size) vanilla instant pudding-and-pie filling
3 cups milk, divided

1 MIX butter, flour, sugar and a handful of nuts. Press into 9- x 13-inch baking dish. Bake at 325°F for 15 minutes. Cool.
2 BEAT cream cheese and sugar until well blended. Spread over crust. Cover with whipped topping.
3 PREPARE each pudding mix with 1-½ cups milk in a separate bowl. Pour chocolate pudding over whipped-topping layer; top with layer of vanilla pudding. Top with additional whipped topping and refrigerate until ready to serve. Top with shaved semisweet baking chocolate. *Serves 16.*

FRUITY PHILADELPHIA FREEZE

Just follow our 3 simple steps:

1 MIX 1 cup finely crushed **cookie crumbs** with ¼ cup butter or margarine, melted. Press onto bottom of 9-inch square pan lined with foil.
2 BEAT 2 tubs (8 oz *each*) **Philadelphia Cream Cheese Spread** until creamy. Gradually add 1 can (12 oz) frozen **juice concentrate**, thawed, beating well. Add 1 tub (8 oz) thawed whipped topping; beat until well blended.
3 POUR over crust. Freeze several hours or until firm. Remove from freezer 15 minutes before serving.

And use the ingredients you have on hand …

What **cookie crumbs** do you feel like?	Try this **Philadelphia Cream Cheese Spread**	Add this **juice concentrate**
chocolate sandwich	strawberry	raspberry
graham cracker	pineapple	lemonade
vanilla wafer	plain	lime
chocolate sandwich	plain	fruit punch

CHOCOLATE PLUNGE

>> **DESSERT DIP**
Mix 1 package (8 oz)
Philadelphia Cream Cheese,
softened, and 1 jar (7 oz)
marshmallow creme
until well blended; cover.
Refrigerate several hours
or until chilled.

Just follow our 2 simple steps:
1 MIX ⅔ cup light corn syrup and ½ cup whipping cream in large microwavable bowl. Microwave on HIGH 1-½ minutes or until mixture comes to boil. Add 1 package (8 oz) Baker's Semi-Sweet Baking Chocolate; stir until chocolate is completely melted.
2 SERVE warm, as a dip, with assorted fresh fruit such as strawberries, apple, cherries, nectarines, pineapple or banana; cookies, cake cubes or pretzels.

Chocolate Plunge is also terrific in the following ways:

CHOCOLATE PEANUT BUTTER PLUNGE
Prepare as directed. Immediately stir in ½ cup peanut butter until blended.

CHOCOLATE RASPBERRY PLUNGE
Prepare as directed. Immediately stir in ¼ cup seedless raspberry jam.

MOCHA PLUNGE
Prepare as directed. Immediately stir in 1 tablespoon instant coffee granules.

4 WAYS WITH SHORTCAKE

Just follow our 2 simple steps:

1 TOSS 2 cups **fruit** with a few spoonfuls of powdered sugar.

2 PLACE **base** on individual serving plates. Finish with **topping** and fruit.

And use the ingredients you have on hand …

What **fruit** do you feel like?	Choose a **base**	Spoon on this **topping**
sliced peeled peaches	angel food cake, cut in slices	Cool Whip Whipped Topping, thawed
raspberries	pound cake, cut in slices	scoops of ice cream
sliced strawberries	biscuits	Cool Whip Whipped Topping, thawed
blueberries	sponge cake, cut in slices	fruit yogurt

BANANA BREAD

2 eggs

3 bananas, mashed

⅓ cup *each* oil and milk

2 cups flour

½ cup *each* Post 100% Bran Cereal and sugar

2 teaspoons baking powder

1 STIR eggs, bananas, oil and milk until well blended.

2 ADD flour, cereal, sugar and baking powder; stir just until moistened. Pour into lightly greased 9- x 5-inch loaf pan.

3 BAKE at 350°F for 1 hour or until done. Cool 10 minutes; remove from pan. Cool completely on rack. *Serves 16.*

RAISIN BRAN MUFFINS

1-¼ cups flour
1 tablespoon baking powder
2 cups Post Raisin Bran
1 cup milk
1 egg, slightly beaten
½ cup applesauce
⅓ cup packed brown sugar
2 tablespoons margarine, melted

>> **KRAFT KITCHENS TIP**
Here we've created a deliciously moist alternative to a traditional muffin by replacing some of the margarine with applesauce.

1 MIX flour and baking powder in large bowl. Mix cereal and milk in another bowl; let stand 3 minutes. Stir in egg, applesauce, sugar and margarine. Add to flour mixture; stir just until moistened. (Batter will be lumpy.)

2 SPOON batter into muffin pan lined with paper liners, filling each cup two-thirds full.

3 BAKE at 400°F for 20 minutes or until golden brown. Serve warm. *Serves 12.*

CLASSIC RICE PUDDING

Just follow our 3 simple steps:

1 MIX 3-½ cups milk, 1 package (6-serving size) cook-and-serve **pudding-and-pie filling** and 1 cup Minute White Rice in medium saucepan.

2 COOK on medium heat, stirring constantly, until mixture comes to boil. Remove from heat.

3 STIR in a handful of **add-ins**. Cover surface of pudding with plastic wrap; cool 10 minutes. Stir. Serve warm.

And use the ingredients you have on hand …

What flavor of **pudding-and-pie filling?**	Try these **add-ins**
vanilla or coconut cream	raisins or sweetened dried cranberries
chocolate	semisweet chocolate chunks or chips
butterscotch or banana cream	toasted chopped pecans and/or sliced bananas
vanilla	chopped apple and/or dash of cinnamon

Rice Pudding with Sweetened Dried Cranberries

FRUIT CRUMBLE

Just follow our 3 simple steps:

1 MIX ½ cup (half 8-oz tub) **cream cheese spread** and 2 cups crushed **cookies** with fork until mixture resembles coarse crumbs. Do not overmix.

2 SPOON **fruit** into pie plate or individual baking dishes; sprinkle with cookie mixture.

3 BAKE at 400°F for 12-15 minutes or until lightly browned. Serve warm.

And use the ingredients you have on hand …

Try this flavor **cream cheese spread**	Use these crushed **cookies**	Spoon In this **fruit**
strawberry	vanilla wafers	chopped peeled fresh peaches or chopped canned peach slices
honey nut or apple cinnamon	oatmeal raisin	canned apple pie filling
plain	oatmeal	chopped peeled fresh pears or chopped canned pear slices
pineapple	gingersnaps	chopped dried tropical fruit mix

QUICK NILLA BANANA PUDDING

Just follow our 3 simple steps:
1 PREPARE 2 packages (4-serving size *each*) vanilla instant pudding-and-pie filling as directed on package for pudding, using only 3 cups milk.
2 SPOON ½ cup of the pudding onto bottom of large serving bowl. Top with Nilla Wafers, a generous layer of sliced bananas and ⅔ cup pudding. Stand wafers around outside edge of dish. Repeat layers twice; top with layer of pudding. Cover.
3 REFRIGERATE at least 3 hours to soften wafers. Just before serving, spread 2 cups thawed whipped topping over pudding. Top with additional banana slices, if desired.

BAKER'S ONE-BOWL BROWNIES

4 squares Baker's Unsweetened Baking Chocolate
¾ cup butter or margarine
2 cups sugar
3 eggs
1 teaspoon vanilla
1 cup flour
1 cup coarsely chopped pecans

1 LINE 9- x 13-inch baking pan with foil extending over edges to form handles. Grease foil.

2 MICROWAVE chocolate and butter in large microwavable bowl on HIGH 2 minutes or until butter is melted. Stir until chocolate is completely melted. Add sugar; stir until well blended. Add eggs and vanilla; mix well. Stir in flour and pecans until well blended. Spread into prepared pan.

3 BAKE at 350°F for 30–35 minutes or until toothpick inserted in center comes out with fudgy crumbs. Do not overbake. Cool in pan. Lift out of pan onto cutting board. Cut into squares. *Makes 24 brownies.*

>> ROCKY ROAD BROWNIES
Prepare batter as directed; spread into pan. Sprinkle with 1 cup Baker's Semi-Sweet Chocolate Chunks or Chips. Bake as directed. Immediately sprinkle with a few handfuls miniature marshmallows, chopped pecans and Baker's Semi-Sweet Chocolate Chunks or Chips.

NANAIMO BARS

>> MINTY NANAIMO BARS
Prepare as directed, adding
a few drops green food
coloring and 1 teaspoon
peppermint extract to
pudding mixture.

2 cups crushed chocolate sandwich cookies

1 cup coconut or chopped nuts

½ cup butter or margarine, melted

1 package (4-serving size) vanilla instant pudding-and-pie filling

⅓ cup *each* butter or margarine, softened, and hot water

2 cups powdered sugar

4 squares semisweet baking chocolate, chopped

1 tablespoon butter or margarine

1 MIX cookie crumbs, coconut and ½ cup melted butter. Press firmly onto bottom of 9-inch square pan. Refrigerate until ready to use.

2 BEAT pudding mix, ⅓ cup softened butter and hot water. Add powdered sugar; beat until well blended. Spread over crust. Refrigerate 2 hours or until filling is set.

3 MICROWAVE chocolate and 1 tablespoon butter on HIGH for 1 minute. Stir until chocolate is completely melted. Spread over pudding layer; refrigerate until set. Cut into bars to serve. Store leftover dessert in refrigerator. *Makes 16 bars.*

CHOCOLATE BLISS COOKIES

1 package (8 oz) Baker's Semi-Sweet Baking Chocolate
¾ cup firmly packed brown sugar
¼ cup butter, softened, or margarine
2 eggs
1 teaspoon vanilla
½ cup flour
¼ teaspoon baking powder
1 package (8 oz) Baker's Semi-Sweet Baking Chocolate, coarsely chopped
   or 1-½ cups Baker's Semi-Sweet Chocolate Chunks
2 cups chopped walnuts

1 MICROWAVE 8 squares chocolate in large microwavable bowl on HIGH 2 minutes. Stir until chocolate is completely melted. Add sugar, butter, eggs and vanilla; stir with wooden spoon until well blended. Add flour and baking powder; mix well. Stir in chopped chocolate and walnuts.
2 DROP scant ¼ cupfuls of dough onto ungreased baking sheets.
3 BAKE at 350°F for 13–14 minutes or until cookies are puffed and feel set to the touch. Cool 1 minute; remove from baking sheets. Cool completely on wire racks. *Makes about 18 large cookies (one cookie per serving).*

>> **KRAFT KITCHENS TIPS**
To make smaller cookies: Mix dough as directed. Drop by heaping tablespoonfuls onto baking sheets. Bake at 350°F for 12-13 minutes. Makes about 30 smaller cookies.

If omitting walnuts, increase flour to ¾ cup to prevent cookies from spreading. Makes about 15 large cookies.

JUMBO OATMEAL COOKIES

1 cup butter or margarine
1-½ cups firmly packed brown sugar
2 eggs
1 teaspoon vanilla
1-½ cups flour
2-½ cups quick-cooking oats
2 teaspoons baking soda
1 package (12 oz) semisweet chocolate chips
1 cup raisins

1 BEAT butter and brown sugar with electric mixer until light and fluffy.
2 ADD eggs and vanilla; mix well. Add flour, oats and baking soda; mix until thoroughly combined. Stir in chocolate chips and raisins. Drop dough in ¼-cup mounds, 3 inches apart, on greased baking sheets. Flatten each cookie into 2-½-inch circle.
3 BAKE at 350°F for 15–16 minutes or until edges are lightly browned. Cool 5 minutes on baking sheets. Transfer to wire racks to cool completely.
Makes 24 cookies.

SUPER EASY PEANUT BUTTER TREATS

Just follow our 3 simple steps:
1 MIX 1 cup peanut butter, ½ cup sugar and 1 egg until well blended.
2 PICK your favorite variation (see below).
3 BAKE at 325°F for 15–20 minutes or until set. Place on wire racks to cool completely.

Peanut Butter Treats are terrific in the following ways:

SUPER EASY PEANUT BUTTER COOKIES
Prepare peanut butter mixture as directed; stir in a few handfuls chopped white baking chocolate and sweetened dried cranberries. Drop spoonfuls of dough onto baking sheets. Bake as directed.

SUPER EASY PEANUT BUTTER PIE
Prepare peanut butter mixture as directed. Press onto bottom and up inside of 9-inch pie plate. Bake as directed. Meanwhile, prepare 1 package (6-serving size) chocolate cook-and-serve pudding-and-pie filling as directed on package for pie filling. Pour into crust. Refrigerate until set.

SUPER EASY PEANUT BUTTER SQUARES
Prepare peanut butter mixture as directed; press into 8-inch square baking pan. Top with a few handfuls chopped semisweet baking chocolate. Bake as directed. Cool completely before cutting into squares.

>> KRAFT KITCHENS TIP
Depending on your personal preference, use creamy, crunchy or reduced-fat peanut butter in this base recipe.

CHOCOLATE-CHUNK COOKIES

>> CHOCOLATE-CHUNK BARS OR SQUARES

Spread dough in greased foil-lined 15- x 10- x 1-inch baking pan. Bake at 375°F for 18-20 minutes or until golden brown. (Or bake in 9- x 13-inch baking pan 20-22 minutes.) Cool completely on wire rack.

1-¾ cups flour
¾ teaspoon baking soda
¼ teaspoon salt
¾ cup butter or margarine, softened
½ cup granulated sugar
½ cup firmly packed brown sugar
1 egg
1 teaspoon vanilla
1 package (12 oz) semisweet chocolate chunks or chips
1 cup chopped walnuts or pecans

1 MIX flour, baking soda and salt in medium bowl; set aside.

2 BEAT butter and sugars in large bowl with electric mixer until light and fluffy. Add egg and vanilla; mix well. Gradually beat in flour mixture. Stir in chocolate chunks and walnuts. Drop by heaping tablespoonfuls onto ungreased baking sheets.

3 BAKE at 375°F for 11–13 minutes or just until golden brown. Cool on baking sheets 1 minute. Remove to wire racks; cool completely.
Makes about 36 cookies.

CHOCOLATE-CARAMEL BARS

32 caramels
½ cup evaporated milk
1 cup *each* flour and quick-cooking oats
¾ cup firmly packed brown sugar
½ teaspoon baking soda
¾ cup butter or margarine
½ cup *each* Baker's Semi-Sweet Chocolate Chunks or Chips, and walnuts

1 MELT caramels with evaporated milk in small saucepan on low heat, stirring frequently.
2 MIX flour, oats, brown sugar and baking soda in large bowl. Cut in butter with pastry blender or fork until mixture resembles coarse crumbs.
3 PRESS half the oat mixture into 9-inch square baking pan. Bake at 350°F for 10 minutes. Sprinkle chocolate and walnuts evenly over crust; drizzle with caramel mixture. Sprinkle with remaining oat mixture. Bake an additional 20-25 minutes or until golden brown. Cool completely. Cut into bars. *Makes 16 bars.*

>> KRAFT KITCHENS TIP
To melt caramels in the microwave, place caramels and evaporated milk in microwavable bowl. Microwave on HIGH for 2-3 minutes or until caramels are completely melted when stirred.

EASY CEREAL SQUARES

Just follow our 3 simple steps:

1 MELT ¼ cup butter or margarine in large saucepan on low heat. Add 6 cups miniature marshmallows. Cook until marshmallows are completely melted, stirring constantly.

2 ADD 6 cups **Post cereal** and a handful of **add-ins**; mix lightly until cereal is evenly coated with marshmallow mixture.

3 PRESS mixture into 9- x 13-inch pan. Cool; cut into squares.

And use the ingredients you have on hand ...

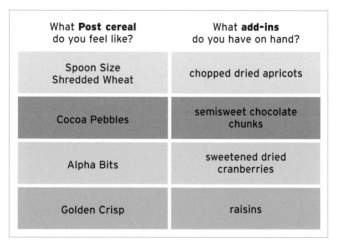

What **Post cereal** do you feel like?	What **add-ins** do you have on hand?
Spoon Size Shredded Wheat	chopped dried apricots
Cocoa Pebbles	semisweet chocolate chunks
Alpha Bits	sweetened dried cranberries
Golden Crisp	raisins

Easy Cereal Squares with Alpha Bits and Sweetened Dried Cranberries

Is there a child anywhere who doesn't have strong feelings about what he thinks tastes good? Personal preferences are all unique, but the Kraft Kitchens have been in the business of pleasing appetites of all ages for quite some time and we know that some of the simplest, most familiar foods enjoy widespread popularity among younger connoisseurs. The recipes featured in the following

Kids' Classics

pages include some of the very best-loved of all these dishes. Consider the appeal of rich and creamy macaroni and cheese with lots of fun variations to suit every youthful appetite, hold-in-your-hand hot-dog roll-ups and some very thick and luscious drinks. You'll also find easy microwave versions of a beloved campfire classic, ice-cream sandwiches the kids can assemble on their own, Gorp squares and even a creamy chocolate fudge with a very surprising secret ingredient. Adults are certain to love them, too – so what are you waiting for?

10 WAYS WITH MAC AND CHEESE

Just follow our 2 simple steps:
1 PREPARE 1 package (7-¼ oz) Kraft Macaroni & Cheese Dinner as directed.
2 STIR IN 1 of the add-ins below to make any of 10 terrific variations.

CHEESEBURGER MAC
Cooked ground beef and a small spoonful prepared mustard.

CHICKEN-AND-BROCCOLI MAC
Chopped cooked chicken and cooked broccoli florets.

CHILI MAC
A few spoonfuls leftover chili. Top with shredded Cheddar cheese.

HAM-AND-CHEESE MAC
Chopped ham and finely chopped green onion.

HOT DOG MAC
Corn and chopped cooked wieners.

PIZZA MAC
Chopped pepperoni and chopped tomatoes. Top with shredded mozzarella cheese.

SAUSAGE MAC
Cooked pork sausage, chopped green pepper and onion.

TACO MAC
Cooked seasoned taco meat. Serve with diced tomatoes and shredded lettuce.

TUNA MAC
Drained, flaked canned tuna and thawed frozen peas.

VEGGIE MAC
A few handfuls of your favorite cooked veggies.

CHEESY HOT DOG CRESCENTS

>> MINI HOT DOG CRESCENTS

>> MINI HOT DOG CRESCENTS
Substitute 16 cocktail wieners for 8 beef franks. Separate dough into triangles; cut each triangle in half lengthwise. Cut each Singles into 4 strips. Assemble and bake as directed.

Just follow our 2 simple steps:
1 SEPARATE 1 can (8 oz) refrigerated crescent dinner rolls into triangles. Top triangles with 4 Kraft Singles, cut in half diagonally, and 8 beef franks; roll up. Place on baking sheet.
2 BAKE at 375°F for 12 minutes or until golden brown. Serve with your favorite condiments.

EASY HOMEMADE MAC AND CHEESE

Just follow our 2 simple steps:
1 COOK 2 cups elbow macaroni as directed on package; drain. Return to hot pan.
2 ADD 1 lb Velveeta, cut up, and ½ cup milk. Cook on low heat until Velveeta is melted, stirring frequently.

>> SHARING OUR EXPERIENCES I like to add extra zip to my Hot Dog Crescents by spreading 1 teaspoon Dijon or prepared mustard, barbecue sauce or ketchup on each dinner-roll triangle before topping with remaining ingredients. Then I prepare them in the usual way. —Tracy, Kraft Kitchens

GORP SQUARES

¾ cup *each* butter or margarine and firmly packed brown sugar

2 tablespoons light corn syrup

3 cups Post Honey Bunches of Oats Cereal, any flavor

1 cup *each* quick-cooking oats, uncooked, and coconut

¾ cup flour

1 teaspoon baking soda

½ cup *each* raisins, chopped apricots and peanuts

1 COOK butter, sugar and syrup in small saucepan on medium
heat until mixture comes to boil, stirring constantly. Remove from heat.
Immediately add to combined remaining ingredients; mix well.
2 PRESS evenly into lightly greased 15- x 10- x 1-inch baking pan.
3 BAKE at 350°F for 12–15 minutes or until golden brown. Cool slightly.
Cut into squares while warm. *Makes 30 squares.*

VELVEETA FUDGE

¾ lb (12 oz) Velveeta, cut up
1 cup butter or margarine
6 squares unsweetened baking chocolate
2 tablespoons light corn syrup
2 lb powdered sugar, sifted
1-½ cups chopped pecans (optional)
1 teaspoon vanilla

1 PLACE Velveeta, butter, chocolate and corn syrup in 3-qt saucepan; cook and stir on medium-low heat until smooth.
2 GRADUALLY add chocolate mixture to sugar in large bowl, beating until well blended. Stir in pecans and vanilla.
3 SPREAD evenly in greased 9- x 13-inch pan; cover. Refrigerate several hours. Cut into squares. *Makes 3-½ lb.*

>> KRAFT KITCHENS TIP Make this fudge ahead of time: Prepare as directed; cool and cut into squares. Wrap tightly. Freeze up to 2 months. Thaw in refrigerator overnight before serving.

JIGGLERS

Just follow our 2 simple steps:

1 STIR 2-½ cups boiling water into 2 packages (8-serving size *each*) or 4 packages (4-serving size *each*) any flavor Jell-O Gelatin in large bowl at least 3 minutes or until completely dissolved. Pour into 9- x 13-inch pan.

2 REFRIGERATE 3 hours or until firm. Dip bottom of pan in warm water for about 15 seconds. Cut into decorative shapes with cookie cutters or cut into 1-inch squares. Lift from pan.

CREAMY JIGGLERS

Just follow our 3 simple steps:

1 STIR 2-½ cups boiling water into 2 packages (8-serving size *each*) any flavor Jell-O Gelatin in large bowl, mixing for at least 3 minutes or until gelatin is completely dissolved. Cool 30 minutes at room temperature.

2 POUR 1 cup cold milk into medium bowl. Add 1 package (4-serving size) Jell-O Vanilla Flavor Instant Pudding & Pie Filling. Beat with wire whisk 1 minute. Quickly pour into gelatin. Stir with wire whisk until well blended. Pour into 9- x 13-inch pan.

3 REFRIGERATE 3 hours or until firm. Dip bottom of pan into warm water for about 15 seconds. Cut into decorative shapes with cookie cutters and lift from pan.

DIRT CUPS

>> **SAND CUPS**
Prepare as directed,
substituting 1 package
(12 oz) vanilla wafers and
Jell-O Vanilla Instant
Pudding & Pie Filling
for chocolate cookies
and pudding.

Just follow our 3 simple steps:
1 CRUSH 1 package (16 oz) chocolate-sandwich cookies; set aside.
2 POUR 2 cups cold milk into large bowl. Add 1 package (4-serving size) Jell-O Chocolate Instant Pudding & Pie Filling. Beat with wire whisk 2 minutes. Stir in 1 tub (8 oz) whipped topping and half the crushed cookies.
3 PLACE about 1 tablespoon of the remaining crushed cookies in each of 8-10 (7 oz) paper or plastic cups. Fill cups about three-quarters full with pudding mixture. Top with remaining crushed cookies. Refrigerate until ready to serve. Garnish with gummy worms, if desired.

HONEY MAID S'MORES

Just follow our 3 simple steps:
1 BREAK 1 milk chocolate candy bar into 4 pieces; set aside.
2 PLACE 4 Honey Maid Honey Grahams on microwavable plate. Top each with 1 chocolate piece and 1 marshmallow.
3 MICROWAVE on HIGH 15-20 seconds or until marshmallow puffs. Top each with second honey graham; pressing slightly. Serve immediately.

COOKIE SANDWICHES

Just follow our 2 simple steps:

1 SPREAD **cookies** with softened **ice cream**; top each with second cookie.

2 ROLL or lightly press edges into **dippers**. Freeze 4 hours or until firm. Wrap individually in plastic wrap. Store in freezer up to 1 month.

And use the ingredients you have on hand …

What **cookies** do you feel like?	Choose an **ice cream** flavor	And now for the **dippers**
chocolate chip	mint-chocolate chip	miniature chocolate chips
oatmeal	vanilla	raisins
chewy chocolate chip	chocolate chip cookie dough	chocolate sprinkles
peanut butter chocolate chip	chocolate	chopped peanuts

WIND CHILLS

Just follow these 2 simple steps:

1 PLACE 1 qt (4 cups) **frozen yogurt**, softened, ¼-½ cup fat-free milk and 8 **cookies** in blender container; cover. Blend until smooth, occasionally stopping blender to scrape down side of container. Add an extra couple spoonfuls of milk, if the mixture is too thick.

2 POUR into 4 glasses. Serve immediately.

And use the ingredients you have on hand …

What flavor **frozen yogurt** do you feel like?	What **cookies** do you have on hand?
vanilla	Oreo Chocolate Sandwich
chocolate	chocolate chip
vanilla	peanut butter sandwich
strawberry	Raspberry Fig Newtons

Index

NOTES

Recipes everyone liked:

_____

_____

_____

_____

_____

_____

_____

_____

_____

_____

_____

_____

_____

_____

_____

_____

_____

_____

_____

NOTES

Recipes I'd like to try:

NOTES

My favorite tips:

_____

_____

_____

_____

_____

_____

_____

_____

_____

_____

_____

_____

_____

_____

_____

_____

_____

_____

_____

_____

_____

A LifeGuide® Bible Study

RAYER
An Adventure with God

12 studies
for individuals or groups

David Healey

With Notes for Leaders

InterVarsity Press
Downers Grove, Illinois

InterVarsity Press
P.O. Box 1400, Downers Grove, IL 60515-1426
World Wide Web: www.ivpress.com
E-mail: mail@ivpress.com

InterVarsity Press® is the book-publishing division of InterVarsity Christian Fellowship/USA®, a student movement active on campus at hundreds of universities, colleges and schools of nursing in the United States of America, and a member movement of the International Fellowship of Evangelical Students. For information about local and regional activities, write Public Relations Dept., InterVarsity Christian Fellowship/USA, 6400 Schroeder Rd., P.O. Box 7895, Madison, WI 53707-7895, or visit the IVCF website at <www.ivcf.org>.

Cover photograph: Dennis Flaherty

ISBN 0-8308-3053-7

Printed in the United States of America ∞

P	17	16	15	14	13	12	11	10	9	8	7	6	5	4	3	2	1
Y	16	15	14	13	12	11	10	09	08	07	06	05	04	03	02		

Contents

Getting the Most Out of
Prayer

A little research would reveal that most Christians (if they were being honest) find prayer hard. We know that we could pray more, or more sincerely, or less selfishly, than we do now. There are books, retreats and conferences to help us. Most are about *how* to pray, but one of the most important things we can learn from the examples of prayer in the Bible is *why* we pray. If we understood a little more of the importance of prayer in the outworking of God's plans and in the way it can change us, maybe we would pray differently. One of the best ways to learn about prayer is to read and hear the prayers of the Bible. Here are some of the things we can discover as we do this.

Prayer Has Variety
One of the striking things about the Bible's prayers is their variety. Thanksgiving in the face of conflict and difficulty are recurrent themes in Psalms and Acts, and the central focus of Mary's prayer. Repentance, inevitable when men and women become intimate with a holy God, recurs regularly, particularly in the great intercessory prayers of Abraham, Moses, Daniel and Nehemiah. Praying for others through intercessory prayer (the main theme of studies one through six) is balanced with heartfelt prayers about their own needs. Prayer for personal circumstances is real, stark and honest in the prayer of Hannah.

Prayer Is Communication
Biblical prayers underline that prayer has at its heart two-way communication with God. Prayer and Bible study are where we talk to God *and* listen to him, discovering his purposes for the world and those around us—purposes always consistent with his revelation to

us in Scripture. By praying we embark on an adventure to become more involved in the outworking of God's plans. Prayer is not popularly understood to be part of the process of us being made more like Christ. But in many of the examples we will study, those who prayed were part of the way in which God answered their prayers. Nehemiah's prayer (study three) commences with his concern about Jerusalem and ends with him asking for the resources to rebuild the city walls. Nehemiah was changed through his own prayer, as was the city and the people who lived there. Prayer is both part of God involving us in his plans, and us being remade in his likeness.

Prayer Is Important
We are told to make disciples of all nations. An essential part of missions is prayer—yet praying for others (intercession) is often one of the weakest areas of our prayer lives. Satan longs to discourage us from praying and loves to make us guilty about our prayerlessness. We are fed the lie that we have to be someone with a "ministry of prayer" before we ever pray beyond our own daily concerns. In the end the devil wants us to believe that our prayers will do nothing significant. But God longs for us to pray, however we can. Impressive-sounding prayers are not necessary. Read aloud the prayers in some of the studies, and see how long they take you. Count the number of big words. You will be surprised how few there are. Prayer need not be complicated to be significant, and it is the privilege and responsibility of all of us.

The Bible shows us ordinary people, in all their weakness, fear and confused motives, being involved in God's purposes for people, nations and ultimately the world. We can get alongside them and understand a little of why they prayed and how they saw God. We see people like us being drawn more into the purposes of God, beginning to want more of what he wants and seeing more of the world as he does.

Growing in Prayer
Each study has at its end both a suggestion for prayer and an idea with which you can try to apply what you have been learning in your

prayer life. You will get the most out of these studies if you try the suggestions either in your own prayer life or with a group.

The background reading suggested in the leader's notes is optional, but it will help you (whether or not you are a leader) in understanding both the background to the passage and some of the difficult issues that prayer opens up, as well as help you lead the study better.

God knows that we can all find prayer difficult. Remind yourself (and others) that God forgives our failings and helps us to start afresh time and time again.

Viewed biblically, the adventure of prayer is meant to involve all of us. But it is not an over-glamorized, Hollywood-style adventure. It demands hard work, commitment and perseverance. It will be high risk, at times painful, always unglamorous and possibly very costly. And we will have to learn on the job until we meet Christ face to face, when it will all be different. But it is an adventure where we journey hand in hand with the one who went to the cross and prays, day in, day out, at the right hand of the Father *for us.*

Suggestions for Individual Study

1. As you begin each study, pray that God will speak to you through his Word.

2. Read the introduction to the study and respond to the personal reflection question or exercise. This is designed to help you focus on God and on the theme of the study.

3. Each study deals with a particular passage—so that you can delve into the author's meaning in that context. Read and reread the passage to be studied. The questions are written using the language of the New International Version, so you may wish to use that version of the Bible. The New Revised Standard Version is also recommended.

4. This is an inductive Bible study, designed to help you discover for yourself what Scripture is saying. The study includes three types of questions. *Observation* questions ask about the basic facts: who, what, when, where and how. *Interpretation* questions delve into the meaning of the passage. *Application* questions help you discover the implications of the text for growing in Christ. These three keys unlock the treasures of Scripture.

Write your answers to the questions in the spaces provided or in a personal journal. Writing can bring clarity and deeper understanding of yourself and of God's Word.

5. It might be good to have a Bible dictionary handy. Use it to look up any unfamiliar words, names or places.

6. Use the prayer suggestion to guide you in thanking God for what you have learned and to pray about the applications that have come to mind.

7. You may want to go on to the suggestion under "Now or Later," or you may want to use that idea for your next study.

Suggestions for Members of a Group Study

1. Come to the study prepared. Follow the suggestions for individual study mentioned above. You will find that careful preparation will greatly enrich your time spent in group discussion.

2. Be willing to participate in the discussion. The leader of your group will not be lecturing. Instead, he or she will be encouraging the members of the group to discuss what they have learned. The leader will be asking the questions that are found in this guide.

3. Stick to the topic being discussed. Your answers should be based on the verses which are the focus of the discussion and not on outside authorities such as commentaries or speakers. These studies focus on a particular passage of Scripture. Only rarely should you refer to other portions of the Bible. This allows for everyone to participate in in-depth study on equal ground.

4. Be sensitive to the other members of the group. Listen attentively when they describe what they have learned. You may be surprised by their insights! Each question assumes a variety of answers. Many questions do not have "right" answers, particularly questions that aim at meaning or application. Instead the questions push us to explore the passage more thoroughly.

When possible, link what you say to the comments of others. Also, be affirming whenever you can. This will encourage some of the more hesitant members of the group to participate.

5. Be careful not to dominate the discussion. We are sometimes so eager to express our thoughts that we leave too little opportunity for others to respond. By all means participate! But allow others to also.

6. Expect God to teach you through the passage being discussed and through the other members of the group. Pray that you will have an enjoyable and profitable time together, but also that as a result of the study you will find ways that you can take action individually and/or as a group.

7. Remember that anything said in the group is considered confidential and should not be discussed outside the group unless specific permission is given to do so.

8. If you are the group leader, you will find additional suggestions at the back of the guide.

1

Conversing with God
Abraham

Focus on Jesus.

If we are honest, many of us only pray with passion when faced with a crisis—exams, big career decisions, suffering or tragedy. In such times of prayer we may discover God in a new way and find almost tangible comfort. But sometimes God may *seem* silent—perhaps distressingly so.

GROUP DISCUSSION. Misunderstanding frequently damages relationships. How can face-to-face conversations help reconcile those whose relationships are fractured?

PERSONAL REFLECTION. Think of a time when you—or someone you know well—struggled to understand God. What place did prayer have in helping you—or them—understand God better?

In this story Abraham finds God telling him about a crisis that will soon overtake the city in which his nephew lives. A remarkable conversation then follows that enlarges Abraham's understanding of God. *Read Genesis 18:16-33.*

---

1. From the evidence in the passage, describe the relationship that existed between Abraham and God. *Talk openly, express.*

How did the sort of relationship they had affect the way God behaved toward Abraham?

Wanted abr to know, all things God will do.

2. How we pray and what we pray for usually reflects, in some way, our deepest desires. In this story, what do you think Abraham was most concerned about?

the people, Not being righteous

3. In verses 16-17 God appears to initiate the conversation with Abraham, and in verse 33 he ends it. In what ways have you experienced God prompting you to pray or letting you know that you have prayed enough about something?

Lost

4. What motivates you to pray for other people, especially those who do not follow Christ? *Lost - No direction.*
Duration

Rt place @ Rt Time.

5. Abraham refers several times to the fact that God appears to want to simultaneously destroy the righteous and the wicked (vv. 23-24, 28-32). Why do you think he keeps questioning God about this?
Phone call - witness them - seed planted.
take hand of God.

6. An intercessor is someone who prays for those deserving of God's <u>judgment</u>. Looking at the example of Abraham, what are some of the qualities we might expect an <u>intercessor</u> to have?

Comp - Zeal
mercy = stand in gap

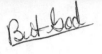 *But God*

7. God is not angry with Abraham for asking questions—even when he appears to question God's justice. How does this fact reassure us when we have to pray in difficult or confusing circumstances?

Don't destroy these people.

Persistant & God. He's God

8. God still went on to destroy Sodom and Gomorrah (you can read the rest of the story in chapter 19). What thoughts and reactions might Abraham have experienced after his conversation with God had ended? *Pray LORD if only 10 righteous.*

Sodom + Gommorah

9. This passage highlights a further aspect of prayer that we easily forget—God may speak to us in prayer. How have you experienced God guiding and prompting you in prayer or changing you through prayer? *Some may go thru = pastor to come to you + go thru problem storm w you*

Humble position. Its all about God.

10. Looking back over the passage, summarize what changed as a result of Abraham's encounter with God. Why did these changes occur? *Show us what*

Ask God to show you how he might want you to deepen your knowledge of him as you reflect on this and other passages.

Now or Later

Set aside a brief time to listen to God by meditating on a passage of Scripture. (You might decide to do this every day for a week, perhaps looking at a series of passages.) Keep a record of what God shows you.

2

Discovering God's Will
Moses

Sometimes we may wonder if prayer changes anything. We may ask, "If God has his plans and will work out his purposes, do we really need to pray?"

GROUP DISCUSSION. What different kinds of things can we pray for people who do not know Christ?

PERSONAL REFLECTION. When you talk to God about friends or family, what do you normally say to him about them?

In this passage we see Moses praying for people who deserve God's judgment—a type of prayer known as intercession. Both Abraham and Moses are intercessors—people who pray in this way. Moses' intercessory prayer has a different (although equally significant) outcome than Abraham's prayer. Moses' prayer changed what happened to Israel. This study helps us to understand how important payer is in God's plans for other people. *Read Exodus 32:1-14.*

---

1. Describe the events leading up to the creation of the golden calf.

Just

14. ~~Israel willfully break~~ Cov. *Prayer*
Keep the Sabbath — a prepetual Cov.

Why do you think Israel made a golden calf to worship?
— a god

40 years

lost their focus.

2. Describe God's response to the Israelites' worship of the golden calf
(vv. 7-10, 12).

Corrupted themselves.
Moses delayed coming down from Mt. Siani..
we don't know what has become of Him

3. It is clear from a passage like this that God is angry about sin and,
rightly, will judge people who reject him. How should knowing this
affect the way you pray for people?

Merciful & good God.
Abr. obeyed God = promise you gave to Ab
follow leader.

4. What does the passage show us both about Moses' character and
what was most important to him as an intercessor? Leadership
Stood in Gap for the people.
he talked to God for His people.

5. If you were Moses, given the actions of the Israelites as described in
verses 1-6, how would you have responded to God's offer in verse 10
to make you a "great nation"? would gods she so def us.

6. Verse 11 shows Moses' reaction to God's command to "stand aside"
in verse 10. What internal conflicts or divided loyalties might Moses
have felt as he spoke to God? Your people
God's wrath burned & him.
He wanted to consume them.

7. What personal risk(s) does Moses' prayer involve?

8. Moses asks God not to destroy the children of Israel (vv. 11-13), reminding God of his promises in Scripture. Why do you think he reminded God about what God had done in the past?

Bec they had been in Egypt 400 years
Rember Abraham.
Israel = Inherit o Land.

9. What caused God to choose an alternative course of action (v. 14) to that which he originally proposed to do in verse 10?

Inherit Land forever

10. Summarize what the passage teaches about the importance of prayer and its potential to change situations.

11. One of the great things we learn about God in this passage is his willingness to show mercy. Who do you need to ask God to show his mercy to? *bec. We are Dust*

Some people you know need to learn of and experience God's mercy. Ask Jesus to show you who they are, and spend some time praying for them.

Now or Later

Make a list of people for whom you do (or can begin to) pray regularly. If you don't already, keep a note of how you pray for them, any answers to prayer and if what you pray for them changes over time.

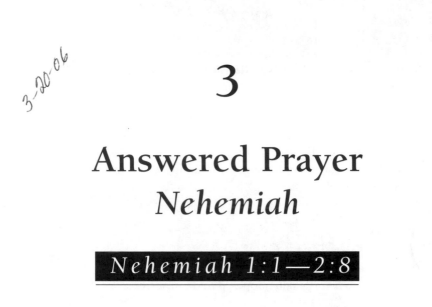

3

Answered Prayer
Nehemiah

Nehemiah 1:1—2:8

At some point in their lives many Christians are tempted to ask God "Why aren't my prayers answered?" though when we do so we may *actually* mean "Why aren't they answered in the way that I want?" However he answers, he always answers in accordance with his will. Sometimes God answers "no," and the Bible gives some reasons why. Frequently he answers "yes," but not instantly. And at other times God may first need us to be prepared to be part of the answer before he will respond to our prayers.

GROUP DISCUSSION. How does what you feel about something or someone affect the way you pray?

PERSONAL REFLECTION. In what ways have your feelings for someone encouraged or discouraged you in your prayer for them?

Jerusalem, the location of the temple of God, was to the Old Testament believer the center of their devotion (as it is for Jews today). Nehemiah, a Jew in exile, was a senior official in the Persian royal court, strategically placed to be part of the answer to his prayer for the rebuilding of Jerusalem. *Read Nehemiah 1:1—2:8.*

1. Based on what you know from the passage, how did Nehemiah's concerns and motives affect what and how he prayed?

---

2. The news that Nehemiah heard in 1:2-3 drove him to definite action (see 1:4). What sort of news would drive you to pray with the same urgency?

---

3. Look carefully at the lengths of time (1:1; 2:1) over which Nehemiah prayed. Why might Nehemiah have had to (or wanted to) pray for a long time about the issues that concerned him?

---

4. Nehemiah 1:5 shows us the first stage of Nehemiah's prayer. How can focusing on God at the beginning of our prayers enable us to pray with more confidence? *focus on God*

Love + Obeyed

5. Nehemiah's prayer then moves into repentance (1:6-7) when he not only confesses his own sin but also his people's wrongdoing. Why, when praying about Jerusalem, might he have felt the need to repent personally as well as identify with the sin of others? *How long. Remind God who he is.*

---

6. Nehemiah referred to God's promises and previous dealings with the children of Israel (1:8-10) as part of his prayer. In what ways do your knowledge of God's actions and character affect the way you pray?

---

7. Nehemiah 1:11 and 2:4 give us an understanding of how Nehemiah saw God in control of the circumstances he faced. How does our understanding of God's sovereignty affect the way we pray for situations?

_____

8. In 1:11—2:8 we see Nehemiah taking steps to tackle the problem of Jerusalem's walls being broken down (1:3). In light of the enormous human and practical odds Nehemiah was up against, what do you think gave him confidence to embark on the task God had given him to do?

_____

9. Nehemiah's fear in 2:2 indicates the risks he was taking in approaching the king on this issue. Why do you think Nehemiah was allowed to speak and ask for help?

_____

10. What does Nehemiah's request show us about his thinking and prayer prior to his audience with the king?

_____

11. How can Nehemiah's example help your prayer life?

Ask God to help you focus afresh on what he has revealed of himself in the Bible and to help you to use that understanding when you pray.

Now or Later

Try writing down what you usually pray for each day, and think of any practical ways in which you might be part of the answer to your prayers.

4

Prayer &
Spiritual Conflict
Daniel

Christians often react in one of two extreme ways to spiritual conflict: they either assume everything stems from it (and so become unhealthily preoccupied with it) or effectively ignore it. Seeing spiritual conflict in the way the Bible sees it is essential both for wise Christian living and specifically for thoughtful prayer.

GROUP DISCUSSION. My father-in-law once said to me, "People's prayers have made a real difference." Discuss ways in which you have experienced prayer making a real difference to people or situations.

PERSONAL REFLECTION. *Jeff* Try to recall a time you have felt close to God. What has been the impact of that experience?

This passage gives us a rare insight into how prayer affects what happens in the (usually invisible) arena of spiritual warfare. *Read Daniel 10.*

Servant

1. What does this passage tell you about Daniel's character?

True Jews

2. When God spoke to him, Daniel refused to eat certain foods and mourned for a period of three weeks (vv. 2-3). Why do you think Daniel did this? His ♡

3. How did Daniel's encounter with the heavenly messenger affect him?

4. What do verses 8-9, 15-17 teach us about the way God deals with us?

5. The description of the man Daniel saw in verses 5-6 is very similar to John's description of Christ in Revelation 1:13-15; alternatively, the "man" may have been an angel. Even though Daniel had received a visit from a heavenly being before, this was still a very unusual occurrence. Why do you think God went to this length to communicate with Daniel?

6. God speaks to us because he wants us to know him and serve him. But when God speaks we don't always respond with the urgency or seriousness that Daniel did. Why might we be reluctant to respond to God?

7. We often interpret world events on a purely human level. But God reveals to Daniel that there is a spiritual battle going on behind the scenes for his people (vv. 13, 20-21). What evidence is there in the passage about the effect of Daniel's prayer on this unseen spiritual battle?

8. Note that Daniel does not directly fight with the satanic forces referred to ("the prince of the Persian kingdom" [v. 13], "the prince of Persia, . . . the prince of Greece" [v. 20]). How does this reassure us when we think about spiritual warfare?

Fast + Pray.

Manifest Himself

9. Sometimes we find it hard to see how God can be at work in world events. How does what the man (or angel) says in the passage help us to understand God's role in human history?

Fast = Revelation, changes
cleanses,

10. Whatever Daniel prayed about, in some mysterious way it influenced both what happened in the spiritual realm and in history. When do you struggle over what to pray?

11. While we will not always understand what to pray for, how can we try to align our prayers with God's desires?

Ask God to help you to pray more and more in ways that reflect what he wants—that his will would be done, and his kingdom would come.

Now or Later

Decide on two or three world situations that you can to pray about. Try to pray about them regularly, especially for the people at the heart of them.

5

Praying for the Nation
Ezekiel

Ezekiel 22:23-31

Have you ever wondered what Jesus would say about your nation if he walked through its streets today? What would he think about the way the poor were treated, or about your government's international aid programs? And what might he say to the drug users he found hiding in the shadows?

GROUP DISCUSSION. In what ways do you think Christians could exert a greater positive influence on your society than they do at the moment?

PERSONAL REFLECTION. In what ways do you most frequently fail to be Christlike toward other people?

Ezekiel, a priest, was called by God to warn his people of God's judgment. Already humiliated in defeat by the Babylonians, Judah was spiritually bankrupt. Like most of his fellow citizens, Ezekiel lived in exile amidst idolatry and materialism. His people, his nation and its leaders paid lip service to their beliefs but led lives that were far from pleasing to God. The passage is the third of three warnings in chapter 22 alone about the sin of Jerusalem and its people. *Read Ezekiel 22:23-31.*

---

1. The absence of rain (v. 24) is probably a symbol of judgment. God's grace and kindness have been removed from his own people; they now live in a spiritual "desert." What sins have brought about God's judgment?

---

2. Societies and people are interdependent. What we do affects others. How would the moral failure of each of the five groups mentioned in the passage (princes, prophets, priests, officials and people) affect the other four groups?

---

3. The priests would have been the principle intercessors. How would their shortcomings (v. 26) have affected their prayer for the nation?

---

4. We often blame our national leaders. Clearly, from this passage, all groups in society bear responsibility for the state of the nation. How should this affect the way we intercede for and live in our nations?

5. The prophets (those in Old Testament times who revealed God's truth into specific situations) were failing to fulfill their responsibilities (v. 28). What do you think motivated them to behave as they did?

6. What moral qualities do you think the spiritual and secular leaders of a nation should possess?

7. The phrase "stand before me in the gap" (v. 30) is symbolic of intercession in the Old Testament. The absence of an intercessor had catastrophic consequences. Why do you think no one wanted to intercede?

8. How do you think our intercessions (and other types of prayers) can affect world events today?

9. Not finding anyone to take positive action to set the nation back on course (to "build up the wall" as Nehemiah did) is seen by God as a problem as serious as having no intercessor. Alongside prayer, what else is necessary for Christians to be a godly influence on their nation?

10. Christians in some countries feel they can have no impact on the life of their nation because they are so few in number. How can this passage encourage believers in such a situation?

11. How would you like this study to change your prayer life?

Jeremiah 29:7 says, "Seek the peace and prosperity of the city to which I have carried you into exile. Pray to the LORD for it, because if it prospers, you too will prosper." Ask God to show you how you and your church can seek the welfare of the community in which you live, and how to pray more precisely for your nation, its leaders and its spiritual life.

Now or Later

Spend time praying for various national leaders. You might use information from newspapers or their websites to help you pray in a more informed way.

6

Praying for Everyone
Paul

1 Timothy 2:1-8

What was it like to be involved in the early church? Acts tells us what was central to its life: Bible teaching, practical fellowship, the sacraments and prayer. The early believers demonstrated social responsibility, were respected by outsiders and daily saw people come to Christ (Acts 2:42-47). Though many of our churches are blessed with buildings and ministry resources the early church leaders never imagined, we have much to learn from their life together.

GROUP DISCUSSION. In what ways is prayer important in the life of the church? (Use your personal experience as well as what you have learned from studies one through five to help you discuss this.)

PERSONAL REFLECTION. In what ways can praying with other people (one-on-one or in a church service) encourage your personal prayer?

In this passage we find the apostle Paul addressing various issues concerning the church and its worship. Interestingly, Paul addresses the issue of prayer first, as one of primary importance to the early church in Ephesus in which Timothy was involved. The issues Paul discusses also provide us with a framework in which to review what we have studied so far. *Read 1 Timothy 2:1-8.*

---

1. What reasons does Paul give in the passage for the importance of prayer?

---

2. How can the church ensure that prayer has its rightful place in the church's life?

---

3. Apart from giving instruction on prayer, Paul, almost in the same breath, discusses essential Christian doctrines (vv. 4-6). Why is Christian teaching/doctrine important for the practice of prayer?

---

4. Paul encourages his readers to pray for all people but then highlights a particular example (v. 2). For Paul's readers, why do you think prayer for those in authority was an important issue? (You may also want to look at studies three, four and five to help you.)

---

5. Often our prayers are self-centered. But Paul (and the examples of Abraham and Moses in studies one and two) encourages us to be selfless in praying for everyone. How can we learn to pray selflessly?

---

6. How do you think that prayer for leaders and those in authority might lead to us live "peaceful and quiet lives in all godliness and holiness" (v. 2)?

---

7. In verses 3 and 6 Paul underlines that God longs for all to come to know him through Christ—even though many will reject him. What have studies one through six taught you (or reinforced for you) about how to pray for seekers?

8. Why do you think prayer is "good, and pleases God our Savior" (v. 3)? (Draw on what you have been learning in all the studies so far.)

9. Paul emphasizes in verse 8 the godly moral integrity ("holy hands") and unity of believers. In what ways can our lack of holiness undermine our prayer?

10. Think about the qualities you have seen in the biblical characters you have studied. What aspects of character are common to these intercessors?

11. What qualities would you most like to have?

Spend some time in quiet reflection on how you might need to change to be able to pray for others more selflessly.

Now or Later

Ask God to teach you how to pray—to help you in the aspects of prayer and praying in which you need to grow.

7

Relying on God
David

Psalm 5

Feeling betrayed, persecuted or fearful are common human experiences, and Christians are no more immune from them than anyone else. Attempting to live faithfully for Christ in the world will bring its own share of opposition and even persecution. How do we pray in these circumstances? Our natural reaction may be fear or anger. Should these feelings shape our prayer?

GROUP DISCUSSION. How do you think serious external pressure, opposition or persecution affects Christians' prayer?

PERSONAL REFLECTION. Think about times when you have been put under—or put yourself under—pressure and how it might have affected the way you prayed.

This is one example of a prayer said in the face of opposition, which shows us how the writer focused on God. *Read Psalm 5.*

---

1. Instead of dealing with his enemies by becoming aggressive or planning revenge, David turns to God in prayer. Summarize the requests David makes of God.

2. David is clearly accustomed to beginning his day with prayer (v. 3). What are the benefits of doing this?

3. When we face aggression or opposition, how can what we know about God give us the confidence to face such situations?

4. David is confident that God hears his prayer (v. 3). What does David know about God that explains his confidence?

5. List the characteristics of the wicked and the righteous from David's descriptions in the passage.

6. Read verses 4-6 and 10. How might David's understanding of God's judgment on his present or future enemies have affected the way David dealt with them?

7. While David clearly sees his enemies as the source of his problems, he sees their sin to be at the heart of their rebellion against God (v. 10). How can this perspective help us to pray for those who oppose us or persecute us because of our faith?

8. How might David's description of God's view of evil (vv. 4, 10) help us when we feel like blaming God for pain or persecution?

---

9. David clearly saw God as his source of refuge (v. 11), protection (v. 11), blessing (v. 12) and shield (v. 12). In what ways do you think David's awareness of God as the provider of his protection helped him to remain faithful during the attacks on him?

---

10. What aspects of David's prayer can specifically help you?

Thank God that he is your refuge in times of trouble, and ask him to remind you of this when you feel under pressure.

Now or Later

Think of people (or circumstances) that threaten or pressure you. Spend some time praying about those situations, trying to focus particularly on God's power and supremacy over the situation (while being realistic about the difficulties). Knowing who God is, how might you behave differently toward (or in) them in coming weeks?

8

Being Honest with God
Hannah

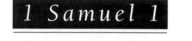
1 Samuel 1

"As you grow in maturity, God's will, God's purposes, God's honor will increasingly concern you. But however mature you may become, you will never cease to have griefs and joys of your own. If prayer that concerns God's honor is to be called higher prayer, I must make it clear that you must never stop appealing to God about your sorrows and heartaches. Lower prayer, if we adopt such an expression, will be necessary as long as you live. 'Have no anxiety about anything,' writes Paul to the Philippian church, 'but in everything by prayer and supplication with thanksgiving let your requests be made known to God' (Philippians 4:6)."*

GROUP DISCUSSION. In what ways can suffering strengthen a Christian's faith? Particularly discuss ways in which it might cause people to pray differently or discourage them from praying.

PERSONAL REFLECTION. Reread the paragraph at the top of this page. Reflect on how balanced your prayer life is between prayer for your own circumstances and needs, and concern for God's honor, will and wider purposes.

Not only is God interested in big issues such as the morality of a nation, how we treat the poor and whether the gospel is being preached; he is also intimately concerned about every single life. *Read 1 Samuel 1.*

---

1. What evidence is there in the passage of faithful and godly living by Elkanah and his family?

---

2. Many of the prayers studied so far are for other people—leaders, nations and the lost. List the ways in which this story illustrates God's concern for individual believers and their needs.

---

3. We often feel conflict between what we want and what we think God wants, and may have mixed motives when we pray. What internal conflicts or mixed motives might Hannah have experienced as she prayed?

---

4. How do you think the way that God answers our prayer is affected by the purity of our motives?

---

5. Verses 10-16 demonstrate Hannah's honesty in prayer to God. She does not hide her feelings, pain, hurt or desire. In a similar situation, what might prevent us from being this direct with God?

6. It is often hard for us to understand other people's suffering. Eli's blessing in verse 17 is very different in tone from his initial reaction to Hannah in verses 13-14. How and why do his views of her change throughout the story?

7. According to the passage, how did Hannah view the child she was asking for?

8. The child God gave Hannah was Samuel, one of the most significant leaders in Israel's history. How do you understand the relationship between God's purposes and our personal circumstances?

9. Compare verse 18 with verses 6-16. How do you explain Hannah's change of mood and apparent sense of assurance?

10. Verses 21-28 detail the events after Hannah's prayer was answered. However, the actions of Hannah and Elkanah relate back to the promise Hannah made in verse 11. What does this teach us about their character as believers?

11. Sometimes we can be hesitant to take personal requests to God. Looking back over the passage, in what ways does the example of Hannah and her household give us confidence in prayer?

12. When are you hesitant to take personal requests before God?

Give thanks for the example of Hannah, and ask God to help you grow spiritually through your personal circumstances—he they easy or difficult. You may also like to express to God things about your personal circumstances that you have found it difficult to verbalize before.

Now or Later
Silently read and reflect on 1 Samuel 2:1-10, noting particularly any aspects of the passage that encourage you.

*John White, *Daring to Draw Near* (Downers Grove, Ill.: InterVarsity Press, 1977), pp. 85-86.

9

Thanking God
Mary

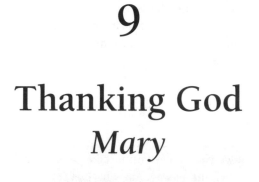

Luke 1:46-55

In a culture where the individual's wants and needs come first, it is easy for Christians to see their rights and freedoms as more important than service and responsibility; to esteem achievement more than obedience and to see being first as more godly than being last. We come to expect God's blessings because we think we merit them.

GROUP DISCUSSION. When do you find it difficult to thank God, and when do you find it easy?

PERSONAL REFLECTION. Spend some time thinking about what or who you thank God for when you pray, and what or who you fail to thank him for.

Mary had few rights—and even fewer privileges—in her culture and her religion. She was probably the last person to expect to be the mother of the Christ. She does not applaud God for choosing her or demand a reward for taking the job on. Instead she prays, conscious of both her God-given significance and the privilege of her calling to be Jesus' mother. *Read Luke 1:46-55.*

---

1. Based on what Mary prayed, what do you discover about what the God she knew was like?

How did Mary think God saw her?

2. How is your relationship with God similar to or different from Mary's?

3. Verses 46-47 tell us that Mary glorified the Lord and rejoiced in her Savior. In what ways can we do this in our prayers?

4. Verse 50 tells us that God's mercy extends to those who fear him. What does it mean to fear God?

How does your fear of God affect the way that you pray to him?

5. Mary thanked God for his choice of her as Christ's mother. However, she also refers to many other actions of God in her prayer. What does this show us about her understanding of God?

6. Imagine you have a Christian friend who feels that God is remote

from his or her situation and has no sense of God's presence in his or her daily life. Consequently, prayer is difficult. How can you help that person to pray?

7. Verses 51-53 contain both warnings and encouragements. What are they?

Which of these do you need to hear and apply to your life?

8. In verses 54-55, Mary speaks of God acting consistently with what he had previously promised. How can the ways that God has fulfilled his past promises (as recorded in the Bible) help us give thanks?

9. Would you like praising and thanking God to play a greater or lesser part in your prayer life than they do already? Explain your answer.

Ask God to help you realize the extent of his love for you and to help you to live a life which more freely expresses your love in words, attitudes and deeds.

Now or Later

Make a list of some things that God has done in biblical history, as well as things that have happened in the last week, that you want to thank him for. Then spend some time in thanksgiving.

10

Blessing Other People
Paul

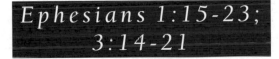
Ephesians 1:15-23;
3:14-21

"Dear Hillary," Beth began. "Thanks so much for your letter. I'm really sorry to hear that the way ahead seems so confusing. I want to reassure you that I do pray for you and that I ask God to clearly guide you as to the next step in your career. I pray that the Lord will bless you."

Beth put her pen down. "Bless?" she thought. "What do I mean? Hillary is in such a difficult situation that I don't know what is best to pray for her. If I just say 'bless,' it sounds like I can't be bothered to think of anything else. What will she think? What does God want me to pray? If I say 'bless,' will he know what I mean?"

GROUP DISCUSSION. When have you had a hard time knowing what to pray for someone?

PERSONAL REFLECTION. If someone says that they will ask God to "bless" you, what would you like that blessing to involve?

It's not easy to know how to pray for a friend. In this passage we see how Paul prays for his friends. *Read Ephesians 1:15-23 and 3:14-21.*

1. What seems to be Paul's motive in praying for those he is writing to?

2. What themes run through Paul's prayers in the two passages?

3. Ephesians 1:15-23 refers back to 1:3-14 (thus the expression "for this reason" in 1:15). Look briefly at that section of Scripture. What does this tell you about the source of Paul's prayer requests?

4. What are some ways that you can use the Bible to help you pray in a specific way for people you know and for your church?

5. There must have been some people in those churches who were hard to get along with. Despite this, Paul gives thanks for them all in 1:16. Why could Paul still do this and pray for them as he did?

6. Look specifically at what Paul prays in 1:17-19. What are some ways in which Paul's prayers might have been answered in Ephesus?

If Paul had been praying for seekers, in what ways would his requests have been different?

7. In the latter part of 1:19 Paul concentrates on God's demonstration of his power through the death and resurrection of Christ. Why do you think he does this?

8. Turn to 3:14-21. How do Paul's words emphasize or illustrate the depth of relationship with God that he wanted to see in the Ephesian believers?

Why might he so strongly stress this depth of relationship (or intimacy) with God?

9. Paul reflects on the love of Christ in 3:16-19 and prays that his readers will experience it profoundly. Why do we need people to pray that for us?

10. Ephesians 3:20 reminds us of God's power and supremacy. How should our understanding of God's ability to change people and circumstances affect the way we pray?

11. Paul clearly longed for the Christians in Ephesus to know God more deeply and prayed accordingly. How, specifically, can Paul's example help us to pray for those around us?

Pray that God will teach you to pray for others with greater insight into what God wants to do in their lives.

Now or Later

Using the central themes of Paul's prayer as a starting point, spend time praying for other Christians that you know.

11

Praying Together
The Early Church

We can pray together in many ways—in a church service, with a friend, alongside people at work or college, or in a prayer meeting. Some of us find these times a great blessing, and some find them very difficult. The experience of the early church was that when they prayed together, the church grew (Acts 2:42). But what were their prayer meetings like?

GROUP DISCUSSION. Some people enjoy praying with other Christians, while others find it a terrifying experience. What contribution to your Christian life has praying with other Christians brought?

PERSONAL REFLECTION. How do you think that praying with someone else does (or could) help you to pray more faithfully?

This passage gives us the opportunity to listen in on one of the early church's prayer meetings, to see how and for what they prayed. *Read Acts 4:23-31.*

1. Peter and John have just been released from prison by the religious authorities for preaching about Christ and performing a miracle. In what way(s) is the early church's response to such persecution surprising?

2. What does the passage teach us about the unity of the believers?

3. How can praying with other Christians build unity in the face of temptation or trial?

4. What aspects of God's character seem to be in the minds of the believers as they pray?

How might concentrating on the character of God have helped the believers to gain perspective on the persecution they faced?

5. Often we perceive evil to have triumphed over good. What can we learn from verses 24-28 to help us understand such situations?

6. Look at the requests in verses 29-30. What do they teach us about

the believers' priorities and attitudes?

7. Not all answers to prayers are dramatic, but the believers' prayer was clearly answered (v. 31). Sometimes we can be surprised by how God answers our prayers. Why do you think this is?

8. Verse 31 tells us that a deeper experience of the Holy Spirit enabled the church to be bold in its evangelism. How does this compare with what Christians often desire from their experience of the Holy Spirit?

9. What do you find difficult about praying with others?

10. What can Christians do (or stop doing) to help each other feel more at ease when praying together?

Pray about any difficult situations you are facing, especially where boldness is required.

Now or Later
Spend some time thinking about how you pray or can pray with other people. If you do pray with others, how can you help them feel at ease praying with you? If you don't pray with anyone else, consider finding someone to pray with and decide together what you can pray about.

12

Praying with Confidence
Jesus

Confidence is a vital factor in human relationships. The confidence that we can trust our friends to keep a promise or to help us out in difficult circumstances enables us to feel secure. And more important, it enables our friendships to grow in an environment of openness.

Just should also characterize our relationship with God. Even though we let him down, he wants us to live in the knowledge that he is absolutely reliable. He hears our prayers, longs to answer them in accordance with his will and is totally fair.

GROUP DISCUSSION. What sorts of things hinder Christians from finding intimacy with God?

PERSONAL REFLECTION. What aspects of the character of God and prayer would you most like reassurance about?

Jesus responds to his disciples' request that he teach them to pray. *Read Luke 11:1-13.*

1. What different aspects of prayer can you see within the model that Jesus gave his disciples in verses 2-4?

2. In what ways do the different aspects and emphases in the prayer provide a model for your own prayer life?

3. Why do you think the friend overcomes his initial reluctance to help his neighbor (vv. 5-8)?

4. The friend gives his neighbor "as much as he needs" in answer to his request (v. 8). What does this passage teach us about how and why our prayers are answered?

5. Luke 11:9-10 considers the issue of persistence in prayer. What does it say that persistence in prayer involves?

6. Jesus teaches on prayer because a disciple asks for teaching in verse 1. In Luke 18:1 he reminds them that "they should always pray and not give up." We are all tempted to not pray or stop praying when we should pray. In what practical ways can we resist such temptation?

7. In what ways does this passage help you to be more confident about prayer?

8. What aspects of prayer do you find easier, and what harder? Try and explain why you think that might be so.

9. Studies one through six of this LifeGuide concentrate on examples of intercession. What other types of prayer have you learned about in studies seven through twelve?

10. What practical steps do you need to take (individually or as a group) to develop your prayer life?

Commit yourself to God by offering a prayer like the following: "Dear God, help me to know that you long for me to communicate with you, and that it is your delight to lead me deeper into your love and purposes. Forgive me when I doubt that. Amen."

Now or Later

Reread line by line the prayer in Luke 11:2-4, pausing between each line to personalize it in some way. For example, after "our Father" you might like to thank God that he has chosen you to be his child.

Leader's Notes

MY GRACE IS SUFFICIENT FOR YOU. (2 COR 12:9)

Leading a Bible discussion can be an enjoyable and rewarding experience. But it can also be *scary*—especially if you've never done it before. If this is your feeling, you're in good company. When God asked Moses to lead the Israelites out of Egypt, he replied, "O Lord, please send someone else to do it"! (Ex 4:13). It was the same with Solomon, Jeremiah and Timothy, but God helped these people in spite of their weaknesses, and he will help you as well.

You don't need to be an expert on the Bible or a trained teacher to lead a Bible discussion. The idea behind these inductive studies is that the leader guides group members to discover for themselves what the Bible has to say. This method of learning will allow group members to remember much more of what is said than a lecture would.

These studies are designed to be led easily. As a matter of fact, the flow of questions through the passage from observation to interpretation to application is so natural that you may feel that the studies lead themselves. This study guide is also flexible. You can use it with a variety of groups—student, professional, neighborhood or church groups. Each study takes forty-five to sixty minutes in a group setting.

There are some important facts to know about group dynamics and encouraging discussion. The suggestions listed below should enable you to effectively and enjoyably fulfill your role as leader.

Preparing for the Study

1. Ask God to help you understand and apply the passage in your own life. Unless this happens, you will not be prepared to lead others. Pray too for the various members of the group. Ask God to open your hearts to the message of his Word and motivate you to action.

2. Read the introduction to the entire guide to get an overview of the

entire book and the issues which will be explored.

3. As you begin each study, read and reread the assigned Bible passage to familiarize yourself with it.

4. This study guide is based on the New International Version of the Bible. It will help you and the group if you use this translation as the basis for your study and discussion.

5. Carefully work through each question in the study. Spend time in meditation and reflection as you consider how to respond.

6. Write your thoughts and responses in the space provided in the study guide. This will help you to express your understanding of the passage clearly.

7. It might help to have a Bible dictionary handy. Use it to look up any unfamiliar words, names or places. (For additional help on how to study a passage, see chapter five of *Leading Bible Discussions*, InterVarsity Press.)

8. Consider how you can apply the Scripture to your life. Remember that the group will follow your lead in responding to the studies. They will not go any deeper than you do.

9. Once you have finished your own study of the passage, familiarize yourself with the leader's notes for the study you are leading. These are designed to help you in several ways. First, they tell you the purpose the study guide author had in mind when writing the study. Take time to think through how the study questions work together to accomplish that purpose. Second, the notes provide you with additional background information or suggestions on group dynamics for various questions. This information can be useful when people have difficulty understanding or answering a question. Third, the leader's notes can alert you to potential problems you may encounter during the study.

10. If you wish to remind yourself of anything mentioned in the leader's notes, make a note to yourself below that question in the study.

Leading the Study

1. Begin the study on time. Open with prayer, asking God to help the group to understand and apply the passage.

2. Be sure that everyone in your group has a study guide. Encourage the group to prepare beforehand for each discussion by reading the introduction to the guide and by working through the questions in the study.

3. At the beginning of your first time together, explain that these studies are meant to be discussions, not lectures. Encourage the members of the group to participate. However, do not put pressure on those who may be hes-

itant to speak during the first few sessions. You may want to suggest the following guidelines to your group.

☐ Stick to the topic being discussed.

☐ Your responses should be based on the verses which are the focus of the discussion and not on outside authorities such as commentaries or speakers.

☐ These studies focus on a particular passage of Scripture. Only rarely should you refer to other portions of the Bible. This allows for everyone to participate in in-depth study on equal ground.

☐ Anything said in the group is considered confidential and will not be discussed outside the group unless specific permission is given to do so.

☐ We will listen attentively to each other and provide time for each person present to talk.

☐ We will pray for each other.

4. Have a group member read the introduction at the beginning of the discussion.

5. Every session begins with a group discussion question. The question or activity is meant to be used before the passage is read. The question introduces the theme of the study and encourages group members to begin to open up. Encourage as many members as possible to participate, and be ready to get the discussion going with your own response.

This section is designed to reveal where our thoughts or feelings need to be transformed by Scripture. That is why it is especially important not to read the passage before the discussion question is asked. The passage will tend to color the honest reactions people would otherwise give because they are, of course, supposed to think the way the Bible does.

You may want to supplement the group discussion question with an icebreaker to help people to get comfortable. See the community section of *Small Group Idea Book* for more ideas.

You also might want to use the personal reflection question with your group. Either allow a time of silence for people to respond individually or discuss it together.

6. Have a group member (or members if the passage is long) read aloud the passage to be studied. Then give people several minutes to read the passage again silently so that they can take it all in.

7. Question 1 will generally be an overview question designed to briefly survey the passage. Encourage the group to look at the whole passage, but try to avoid getting sidetracked by questions or issues that will be addressed later in the study.

8. As you ask the questions, keep in mind that they are designed to be

used just as they are written. You may simply read them aloud. Or you may prefer to express them in your own words.

There may be times when it is appropriate to deviate from the study guide. For example, a question may have already been answered. If so, move on to the next question. Or someone may raise an important question not covered in the guide. Take time to discuss it, but try to keep the group from going off on tangents.

9. Avoid answering your own questions. If necessary, repeat or rephrase them until they are clearly understood. Or point out something you read in the leader's notes to clarify the context or meaning. An eager group quickly becomes passive and silent if they think the leader will do most of the talking.

10. Don't be afraid of silence. People may need time to think about the question before formulating their answers.

11. Don't be content with just one answer. Ask, "What do the rest of you think?" or "Anything else?" until several people have given answers to the question.

12. Acknowledge all contributions. Try to be affirming whenever possible. Never reject an answer. If it is clearly off-base, ask, "Which verse led you to that conclusion?" or again, "What do the rest of you think?"

13. Don't expect every answer to be addressed to you, even though this will probably happen at first. As group members become more at ease, they will begin to truly interact with each other. This is one sign of healthy discussion.

14. Don't be afraid of controversy. It can be very stimulating. If you don't resolve an issue completely, don't be frustrated. Move on and keep it in mind for later. A subsequent study may solve the problem.

15. Periodically summarize what the group has said about the passage. This helps to draw together the various ideas mentioned and gives continuity to the study. But don't preach.

16. At the end of the Bible discussion you may want to allow group members a time of quiet to work on an idea under "Now or Later." Then discuss what you experienced. Or you may want to encourage group members to work on these ideas between meetings. Give an opportunity during the session for people to talk about what they are learning.

17. Conclude your time together with conversational prayer, adapting the prayer suggestion at the end of the study to your group. Ask for God's help in following through on the commitments you've made.

18. End on time.

Many more suggestions and helps are found in *Leading Bible Discussions*, which is part of the LifeGuide Bible Study series.

Components of Small Groups
A healthy small group should do more than study the Bible. There are four components to consider as you structure your time together.

Nurture. Small groups help us to grow in our knowledge and love of God. Bible study is the key to making this happen and is the foundation of your small group.

Community. Small groups are a great place to develop deep friendships with other Christians. Allow time for informal interaction before and after each study. Plan activities and games that will help you get to know each other. Spend time having fun together—going on a picnic or cooking dinner together.

Worship and prayer. Your study will be enhanced by spending time praising God together in prayer or song. Pray for each other's needs—and keep track of how God is answering prayer in your group. Ask God to help you to apply what you are learning in your study.

Outreach. Reaching out to others can be a practical way of applying what you are learning, and it will keep your group from becoming self-focused. Host a series of evangelistic discussions for your friends or neighbors. Clean up the yard of an elderly friend. Serve at a soup kitchen together, or spend a day working on a Habitat house.

Many more suggestions and helps in each of these areas are found in *Small Group Idea Book*. Information on building a small group can be found in *Small Group Leaders' Handbook* and *The Big Book on Small Groups* (both from InterVarsity Press). Reading through one of these books would be worth your time.

Study 1. Conversing with God. Genesis 18:16-33.
Purpose: To discover how God participates with us in setting the agenda for prayer.

General note. Intercession is the main theme of studies one to six, so this passage should help the group to become familiar with the idea of praying for others in this way.

Background note. Around 2000 B.C. Abraham and Sarah are visited by three strangers who are actually the Lord himself and two angels. Abraham and Sarah are promised a child (remarkable given their ages—see Gen 18:11). The visitors are about to depart when this story begins in verse 16.

Group discussion. Every study begins with a question for the group to discuss before the passage is read. These questions are important for several reasons.

First, they help the group to warm up to each other. No matter how well a group may know each other, there is always a stiffness that needs to be overcome before people will begin to talk openly. A good question will break the ice.

Second, group discussion questions get people thinking along the lines of the topic of the study. Most people will have lots of different things going on in their minds (dinner, an important meeting coming up, how to get the car fixed) that will have nothing to do with the study. A creative question will get their attention and draw them into the discussion.

Third, these questions can reveal where our thoughts or feelings need to be transformed by Scripture. That is why it is especially important not to read the passage before the approach question is asked. The passage will tend to color the honest reactions people would otherwise give because they are, of course, supposed to think the way the Bible does. Giving honest responses before they find out what the Bible says may help them see where their thoughts or attitudes need to be changed.

This group discussion question is designed to explore the common human experience that misunderstandings between people, if not dealt with, damage relationships. If we are not careful, it can damage our relationship with God. We may think God is not doing what we expect him to, or we may think we know better. So we stop talking with him; we stop praying and reading the Bible instead of seeking constantly to see things as he sees them.

Question 1. Abraham and God knew each other well. Regardless of Abraham's failings, Abraham is treated as a friend with whom God is prepared to share his plans and purposes. Encourage the group to realize that we are in a similar, privileged position and that as friends of and partners with God he wants us actively involved in his purposes and sharing with him intimately (which we do not always find easy).

Question 2. Look at verses 23 and 25. Note that despite Lot and his family living in the city (one concern), Abraham did not allow his personal involvement to eclipse his longing to see God's justice carried out.

Question 3. The focus of Abraham's prayer shifts from discussing his future child (first part of chapter 18) to God's justice and mercy. God shifts the agenda of Abraham's prayer and also, it appears, prompts him to begin to pray and ends the prayer time. We often approach prayer as if it is our responsibility alone. However, it involves both divine initiative and human response. Abraham may have thought he initiated the conversation with God, but looking back, it is clear that God initiated the conversation. As you discuss the group members' experiences of how God has prompted them to pray or to stop praying about something, bear in mind that God won't tell us to stop praying completely! We are commanded to pray constantly and must always be open to pray for someone or something. An alternative question would be to imagine how Abraham felt as God defined both the beginning and end of his conversation with God and what they talked about.

Question 4. The need to understand why we intercede is essential in evangelism. In intercession we are involved in God's plan for those around us; praying for others involves, at some level, wanting for them what God wants for them.

Question 5. John White comments, "His prayer is not, as some scholars suggest, a mere reflection of the bargaining practices among traders in the East. Abraham has nothing to offer in trade with God. Moreover the stakes are too high. He is not haggling with God. He is desperate to understand" (*Daring to Draw Near* [Downers Grove, Ill.: InterVarsity Press, 1977], p. 19).

Abraham is (reverently and fearfully) probing God's character and justice. He wants to know what God is like and why he is doing this. As a general point on the passage, some in the group may find it difficult to accept the idea that God is not neutral about those who reject him; those who reject his offer of salvation in Christ are under his judgment and are separated from him.

Question 6. Abraham, to risk questioning God, must have been prepared to be selfless. Other characteristics frequently found in intercessors are concern for God's glory and reputation (for example, "Will not the Judge of all the earth do right?" v. 25) and concern for people under God's judgment ("Will you sweep away the righteous with the wicked?" v. 23).

Question 7. That God is willing to be on the receiving end of probing questions should give us reassurance in prayer. This passage also alludes to God's fairness (v. 21) and the fact that he allows the depths of his own nature to be explored and probed by Abraham. This is no far-off God. If sometimes he seems difficult to understand, we are free to express our feelings, even our doubts to him. God can take it!

Question 8. It is often disillusioning for us not to have our prayer answered in the way we expect. John White comments as follows:

> Why did Abraham stop at ten? We may never know. One thing is certain. He was reassured. As each response came back at him, "For the sake of forty I will not do it. . . . I will not do it, if I find thirty there. . . . For the sake of ten I will not destroy it . . ." the image of God was changing in Abraham's eyes. It was no monster that faced him, but the familiar

God of the covenant. Yet somehow God was larger. He was less comprehensible. And, paradoxically, he was a God Abraham understood better than ever before. A familiar God whom yet he scarcely knew. A righteous God whose judgments were past finding out. (*Daring*, p. 21)

Question 9. This is an unusual prayer in the sense that Abraham is literally face to face with God and appears to get immediate responses to his questions. Do not let the unusual circumstances cover up an important general principle about prayer, namely its two-way nature. As the group discusses how God speaks and prompts, bear in mind that God's leading will never be inconsistent with his revealed truth in Scripture, and any decisions, guidance or prompting we think we receive from God must always be weighed against it. While God spoke in a direct, audible way to many biblical figures, because we have the Bible (which they did not, in its complete form) we have constant access to God's words.

Accordingly, his primary way of conveying his truth today is through the Bible; the Bible is described technically as "sufficient," that is, it gives us enough teaching to be able to know God and obey him. Of course, being indwelt by a living God means that we will feel the presence of God, and he will certainly prompt and guide us experientially *but always in ways consistent with the Bible.* There is no encouragement in the New Testament to search for new truth beyond that set down in the Old Testament and in the apostolic teaching which forms what we now call the New Testament (see Jude 3). In the same way that making decisions involves using our minds, under the direction of the Spirit renewing our minds and consciences, growing in prayer and praying more biblically involves having our minds renewed so we *think* more in line with what the Bible says God wants (Rom 12:2, see also *Daring*, pp. 12-13).

Now or later. Christian meditation involves filling our minds with God, for example, reflecting on a passage of the Bible, in contrast to the Eastern mystic or New Age meditation of emptying our minds. If the group agrees to do this exercise, it would be good to agree on one or two passages from the Bible (for example, the passage for the next study) so the group has a focus for its learning. Agree to share together what you have learned the next time you meet.

Study 2. Discovering God's Will. Exodus 32:1-14.
Purpose: To further explore the nature of intercession, the character of an intercessor and the role of intercession in God's purposes.
Background note. Moses, leader of the Israelites, is on Mount Sinai, and the

children of Israel are below, under the leadership of Aaron. It is only recently that the Israelites enthusiastically accepted the terms of God's covenant and promised obedience to his laws.

Group discussion. Depending on the members of the group, you may find that people do not pray for those around them who are unbelievers. (Any discussion may need careful handling if your group contains unbelievers, or you might want to use the suggested personal refection instead.) Try to discover how specific people are in what they pray.

Question 1. We like to worship things and people that we can see and feel—it seems easier than worshiping a supernatural and invisible God. Despite their acceptance of God's laws and a pledge of obedience to them, within weeks the Israelites are breaking their promises to God. They make a replica of the gods they saw in Egypt, desiring the same sort of god to worship as their pagan neighbors. Having a calf (probably a more accurate translation is a "young bull") to worship may have reminded them of the sacred bull of Egypt, Apis, or it may have been a representation of the Canaanite god Baal (Alan Cole, *Exodus*, Tyndale Old Testament Commentary [Downers Grove, Ill.: InterVarsity Press, 1973], p. 214).

Question 2. Contrast their actions with the first commandment in Exodus 20:3.

Question 3. If discussion turns to whether God's judgment is unfair or unnecessary, it is important to note that God would be unjust if he left sin unpunished. Sometimes we think other people deserve God's judgment more than we do and are tempted to look down on them (especially those who do not know Christ) because we feel morally, racially or spiritually superior. Pride affects both the way we pray and the acceptability of our prayers to God.

Question 4. The following qualities are typical of the pattern of Old Testament intercessors: reverent fear of God, boldness, concern for people and a preparedness to take personal risks. Note particularly Moses' concern for God's glory and reputation: "In ancient Near Eastern religions it was believed that gods habitually became angry with their worshipers (for both unknown and unknowable reasons) and lashed out at them. Moses' plea is thus focused on preserving the distinctiveness of Yahweh's reputation" (John H. Walton, Victor H. Matthews and Mark W. Chavalas, *The IVP Bible Background Commentary: Old Testament* [Downers Grove, Ill.: InterVarsity Press, 2000], p. 115).

Question 5. It is possible that by making such an offer to Moses, God is in fact testing Moses' integrity to see if he puts God's purposes first or his own selfish desires.

Question 6. Encourage the group to imagine themselves in Moses' position and to think of his own (perhaps sharply conflicting) desires and loyalties. What might Moses be thinking about? How to rid himself of the troublesome Israelites, his own position as a leader, God's image and reputation on the eyes of the surrounding peoples and God's reaction to his questioning may have all concerned Moses, who would have had to be ruthlessly honest about his own ambitions before he could pray honestly to God.

Question 7. Moses appears to contemplate disobeying God's command in verse 10 (presumably at the risk of his life) in the interests of his people. The situation appears again to reflect the fact that Moses is being tested just as God tested Abraham to see if he really trusted God (Gen 22).

Question 8. Moses could be certain of God's promises on the basis of the limited biblical material he had. His prayer was not based on subjective impressions of what he thought God might want to do, but on what God definitely had said and done. Moses can therefore ask with confidence. The promises and events Moses refers to in verses 12-13 are based on Genesis 12:7; 13:15; 15:5, 18; 17:8; 22:16-18; 26:4; 35:12; Exodus 13:5, 11; 33:1, Numbers 14:13-19; Deuteronomy 9:28 and Joshua 7:9. Indirectly this passage underlines the value of Scripture as a basis for prayer.

Question 9. Try not to get sidetracked into complex discussions on sovereignty and free will in this question. Since God is perfect, he does not "change his mind" because he realizes he has made a mistake—nor just because he feels like it. God's behavior here is explained in human terms so that we can understand it. God embarked on a "different" course of action (for example, showing mercy) from that already proposed (judgment) due to a new factor—the prayer of Moses. Often in the Bible God's warnings and promises are conditional on men's and women's responses (for example, see Jn 1:12)

John, in Revelation, pictures prayers being brought into the presence of God in golden bowls, signifying their great importance to God. Clearly our prayers cannot be the place where we order God around, otherwise he would no longer be God. Here Moses has his views and desires brought into line with what God wants. (In a parallel way in the previous study Abraham discovered more about God.) Moses did not alter God's purpose for the children of Israel but instead carried it out. He began to share God's mind and purpose more, as did Abraham.

Question 10. Discuss, if possible, how the lessons you learn in the group about intercession can be applied practically. How important we see prayer to be in bringing about God's purposes will change the way we pray. Equally, seeing prayer as a place where we learn about God and discover more of his purposes elevates its importance.

Now or later. If you are meeting with a group, encourage them to pray on a regular basis for two or three non-Christian friends. For two or three meetings, discuss how your prayer for the person or situation is changing and what has happened (if anything) as result of your praying for them.

Study 3. Answered Prayer. Nehemiah 1:1—2:8.
Purpose: To discover how our prayers can work together with God's desires for us and for others.
Background note. The story of Nehemiah is a continuation of the story told in Ezra, and begins around 446 B.C. Israel is in exile. Jerusalem was destroyed in 587 B.C., and most Jews were taken off into captivity to Babylon, in the Persian empire. The Jews had been permitted to return to Jerusalem, first between 538 and 516, and then later under Ezra's leadership when attempts to rebuild the walls of Jerusalem were thwarted (Ezra 4:7-23). The rebuilding is ultimately carried out by Nehemiah, permitted as a result of the Persians' policy of religious toleration.

One issue highlighted in this study is that we must be prepared to be used by God to answer our own prayers. The group may need to be reminded that some prayers are not answered for reasons entirely outside of our control or influence. For instance, we may pray for friends to become Christians, but ultimately they have free will and choose whether or not to receive Christ— within the context of divine sovereignty.
Group discussion. This question may bring out very different views of the place of emotion and feelings, which often reflect the personalities of the individuals. Bear in mind that prayer is a command. It is to be done whether or not we feel like it (although that may sometimes be very difficult). But feeling concern can help us to pray and may reflect something of what God feels, if it's in line with God's will. If our prayer life is dry, we may need to pray for enthusiasm. If our practice of prayer is dependent only on feelings, we need to ask for and cultivate the habit of self-discipline.
Question 1. "Like all his people, Nehemiah looked to Jerusalem as his heart's true home and the center round which his life revolved" (John White, *Excellence in Leadership* [Downers Grove, Ill.: InterVarsity Press, 1986], p. 14).

Nehemiah's concern to see Jerusalem rebuilt and restored was not based on nationalism or political ambition. Rather, it was built on a desire to see true worship of his God at its heart, the temple, and on shame that Jerusalem had been humiliated in judgment because of the Israelites' idolatry, materialism and unbelief.
Question 3. Note that the recorded words of Nehemiah would have only

taken a minute or two to pray. We assume they represent a summary of a process of prayer. The month of Kislev (1:1) corresponds to mid-November through mid-December 446 B.C. By the time Nehemiah has audience with the king (2:1), it is the month of Nisan (March-April 445 B.C.). We can only guess what Nehemiah may have gone through over this four-month period and why God wished him to pray for this long period. God may have needed to bring Nehemiah to the point where he was prepared—or felt able—to be involved, or to enable him to reflect for a long time on what was the best plan of action so that he did not rush into a course of action that would fail.

Question 5. Identification is an increasingly difficult concept for people who live in highly individualistic cultures to understand. Western cultures usually place high emphasis on individual responsibility—we blame others, not ourselves, for our nation's ills. In contrast, Nehemiah saw himself to be as responsible as the next person for his nation's troubles.

Question 6. Intercessors frequently return to God's specific promises as a basis for prayer. You may want to explore how much group members use the Bible as part of their prayer lives and let it shape what they pray, as Nehemiah did.

Question 7. Note that Nehemiah not only prays for God's help prior to the encounter with the king (1:11); he prays again in 2:4 when he is talking to him. This indicates his awareness of God's presence with him and his reliance on God. Nehemiah's role as cupbearer (a position requiring great integrity) meant he had access to the king that few others had. His role was to test the king's wine to ensure that it was not poisoned—a common cause of death for leaders in ancient times. Being sad in the king's presence was viewed as disapproval of the king himself and usually resulted in death. So Nehemiah is in a high-risk situation.

Question 8. Nehemiah would have drawn strength from the promises and character of God (1:5-10), the prayers of others (1:11), and possibly the human circumstances he found himself in (1:11). There may have been other factors, such as confidence that God had heard his prayer, but we cannot identify this from the text.

Question 9. Nehemiah's trustworthiness (see note to question 7) might have been a factor in the king's willingness to listen to him.

Question 10. Nehemiah used his mind to the fullest in the planning, for example, deciding in advance to request letters for safe conduct and timber. Normally we think of vision as a very general, even vague, thing. Nehemiah, however, had both a clear vision of what God wanted him to do and a detailed strategy to achieve the task God had set out for him. He also couched his request in language calculated to win him the ear of a Persian king by referring to "the city where my fathers are buried." Persians were very concerned with family ties and paid strict attention to the care of remains of family members (*Bible Background,* p. 473). To ask in this way demonstrates sensitivity to the culture he was exiled in as well as avoids use of politically provocative references to the Jews' homeland and a city with a reputation for being troublesome. Note also that Nehemiah's prayer changed: he moved from a general concern to prayer for specific action, and he initially prayed alone, but by 1:11 others prayed also.

Question 11. Try to get the group to be as practical as possible in their application of the lessons from the passage. One might miss that Nehemiah prayed an enormous amount before setting out on the task God had asked him to do. Often we only pray briefly or only once we are in the midst of the situation that is not working out the way we planned!

Now or later. You could ask the group if they would be willing to share what they have learned by doing this. Praying for a friend to become a Christian may lead them to realize that they could help their friend to study the Bible and thus be used by God to bring about the answer to their prayer.

Study 4. Prayer & Spiritual Conflict. Daniel 10.

Purpose: To examine the relationship between prayer and spiritual warfare.

Background note. The two southern Israelite tribes, called Judah, were conquered by the Babylonians in 586 B.C. Around 605 B.C. Daniel was taken along with other young Jews to work for the Babylonian authorities. From 605 to 536 B.C. the Jews were oppressed by the Babylonians and exiled, Jerusalem being destroyed. Then the Babylonians were overthrown by the Persians. Daniel lived through the exile of seventy years, and the story in chapter 10 occurs around the end of the exile (537 B.C.), when Daniel desires to know what will happen after the seventy years are over. Daniel 10—12 represents an insight into future world events but is rather complex to interpret. (Try not to get involved in discussing complex theologies of the end times.) In brief, many assume that the vision predicts the messianic age (10:14), the future events involving Babylon and Greece (11:2-20), Antiochus and the antichrist (11:21—12:3).

Daniel's vision. A few words of explanation might help with this unusual type of biblical literature. Daniel has a vision, either of God or of an angelic being, the purpose of which is to explain a "revelation"—a message from God (10:1). Why did God speak to him in this way?

Early believers such as Daniel did not have the Bible in its completed form as we do. Part of the way the Bible came to us was through such events as

Daniel's vision and its interpretation. God used the vision to reveal himself both directly to Daniel and ultimately to us through the authoritative biblical record of Daniel's experience. In biblical times (as now) such visionary encounters are rare, as were Abraham's and Moses' "face-to-face" encounters with God.

Daniel's visions had therefore a special status (as did Moses' encounter on Mount Sinai) because they were to form part of God's enduring revelation, now passed on to us in the Bible. The purpose of a vision today (were one to occur) would not be, as Daniel's was, to contribute to the canon of Scripture (which is complete). A contemporary vision would be similar in authority to a statement made by a congregation member exercising the New Testament gift of prophecy in a church today.

Visions must be weighed against Scripture. Visions are, of course, by nature subjective and transient. How you interpret a vision depends on who interprets it; you cannot go back and look again at the vision to see what it depicted. Spiritual experiences like a vision are generally given at God's initiative rather than because people seek them. (See the leader's notes for study five, and Roy Clements's chapter on "Word and Spirit" in *Hear the Word*, ed. John White [Leicester, U.K.: Inter-Varsity Press, 1990].)

Daniel's fall to the ground. While the principal theme of this passage is prayer and spiritual warfare, Daniel's prayer involves a profound spiritual experience: not only did he receive a vision but he went into a trance or altered state of consciousness. However unusual or dramatic, Daniel's experience is incidental to the central meaning of the passage. Christians in your group may disagree about the meaning and validity of spiritual experiences. Some may have had very tangible experiences of the Holy Spirit's work and be enthusiastic for others to enjoy the same. Others may be very suspicious of such events. Some think "experiences" make you in some sense superior as a Christian; others think that such experiences are automatically suspect because they are frequently "emotional." Try to not let the discussion be distracted from studying what the passage says.

Daniel neither sought his experience deliberately nor became preoccupied with it. It happened, but he did not seek the experience for his own sake. His concern was to understand God and his purposes (v. 16). The test of anything we experience should be whether it increases devotion to Christ and Christlikeness—the fruit of anything that is authentically of God. Bear in mind that many biblical characters experienced God in a variety of ways, and we should not seek to stereotype or dictate the way God deals with us on this level. There is no encouragement to seek dramatic spiritual experiences for their own sake, and similarly we cannot expect Christianity to be devoid of experience; it is about a relationship, so we cannot separate the words of God from the breath that carries them.

Question 1. Verses 11-12 and 19 especially underline Daniel's qualities and devotion. In spite of Daniel's remarkable faith and obedience (there is no recorded sin in the life of Daniel, although he was, of course, not sinless), the presence of the Lord rendered Daniel helpless (v. 8). Daniel's personal holiness was no match for God's.

Question 2. If fasting is a new idea for the group, it is usually understood to mean going without food and drink for a period of time. Here Daniel gives up certain food and drink, presumably as a way of humbling himself to reflect a state of mourning and a desire for guidance from God.

Question 4. Note the balance between God demonstrating his power and holiness, with which those present were humbled (vv. 7-8, 15), and the grace of God dealing gently with Daniel (vv. 10, 18) in his weakness. God understands our limitations and consequently protects us from things with which we cannot cope—even direct encounters with God himself that would be too much for us to withstand (see, for example, Ex 33:20-23; 1 Kings 19:11-13).

Question 5. Daniel's previous angelic visitation (Dan 9, around 539 B.C.) involved Gabriel explaining to him that the earthly opposition to his people would be overthrown. The purpose of the vision in 10:1—12:13 is positive assurance for God's people. Why God communicated as he did with Daniel we do not know for sure, but it was probably to demonstrate his strength and power so that Daniel (and those who would read of the vision in years to come) would be reassured. This may have been particularly necessary if the Jewish people believed their identity was going to be destroyed by exile in pagan Babylon. They may have come to doubt that God would work out his purposes for them, and the whole book is written to help them remain faithful to God and to live in hope of future salvation while in exile (vv. 19, 21).

Questions 7-8. This is a very difficult passage to interpret. The following should help you understand the general ideas behind the passage:

☐ Parallel hierarchies of good and evil angelic beings exist in the spiritual realm (I. Howard Marshall et al., eds., *New Bible Dictionary*, 3rd ed. [Downers Grove, Ill.: InterVarsity Press, 1996], p. 358).

☐ Verse 12 indicates that God responded to Daniel's prayer and had come to him because of it.

☐ Unseen spiritual conflict lasted for three weeks (v. 13), which was the same length of time for which Daniel prays and mourns (vv. 2-3).

☐ The expression "the prince of the kingdom of Persia" represents a demonic being (that is, a fallen angel) with a geographical or racial responsibility. Michael (10:21; 12:1) is, in contrast, the divine angel responsible for the Jews. *W arréov augel arc -augel*

☑ Daniel is not fighting the battle directly—no human could. But Christ and the angelic servants of God are involved directly in the spiritual warfare. In prayer we can be caught up in these conflicts, which affect events in the world on a visible level. Ronald Wallace comments, "The heavenly host [angels] in their conflict need the support of earthly intercessors, and the earthly people of God in their conflict need the help of the heavenly host" (*The Message of Daniel* [Downers Grove, Ill.: InterVarsity Press, 1979], pp. 178-79).

Question 9. Look particularly at verses 12-14 and 19-21. If you find this question difficult to discuss, start by listing things that God does in the passage, and try to work out what the practical implications were for Daniel, his generation and those who have read the story subsequently. Some clues are: God explains things to us (vv. 12, 14); God is active behind the scenes, although we may not see this (v. 13); God reassures us in the midst of conflict (v. 19); he tells us the truth (v. 21); he conquers evil (v. 21).

Question 11. From the wider context of Daniel's life, as an experienced office-holder in government for decades, he would have had more insight than most into the political circumstances of his times and their implications for the future of the Jews. It is highly likely that he used that insight to pray generally for his nation.

To know the mind of God we need to know the Bible and prayerfully apply its wisdom under the guidance of the Spirit. We pray obediently in accordance with our limited understanding. Given that fact, note that Daniel prayed in 10:2 without apparently understanding what was going on. Often we will pray like this and will need to pray for wisdom about *how* to pray. At times we may only understand the significance of our prayers after the event, but specific insight from God as to how to pray will always be consistent with Scripture's teaching.

Study 5. Praying for the Nation. Ezekiel 22:23-31.
Purpose: To examine the significance of prayer and leadership in national life.
Background note. Ezekiel would have been taken into exile with many of his people by the Babylonians around 597 B.C. He was called to be a prophet around 593 B.C., at a time when the people of God were surrounded by excessive idolatry and materialism in Babylon—a contrast to his upbringing in the temple as the child of a priest. (The studies on Daniel and Nehemiah provide more historical detail.)

There are five types of leaders or groups described in the passage (depending on the Bible version[s] your group uses). To help deal with issues arising in the passage, the following notes may be helpful regarding each type of leader or group.

☐ "Princes" (v. 25 NIV) refers to the members of the royal household; an alternative translation is "prophets" (NASB) (see also v. 28). There is debate by the commentators as to which is the correct translation. Using either does not significantly alter the general meaning of the passage.

☐ "Priests" (v. 26) were those who officiated in the temple and interceded for the people.

☐ "Officials" (v. 27 NIV) or "princes" (NASB) refers to the politicians or ruling class/nobility.

☐ "Prophets" (v. 28) were those who claimed to speak for God (see note on v. 25).

☐ "People of the land" (v. 29) were those with full citizenship rights; they could oppress those without such rights; for example, aliens (immigrants) or slaves.

Prophets and prophecy. In case of confusion, note the differences between prophets and prophecy in the Old and New Testament. In the Old Testament the true prophet of God, such as Jeremiah, spoke verbally inspired, infallible prophecy with an objectivity which the type of prophecy Paul refers to 1 Corinthians 14 does not possess (see below). In the New Testament the equivalent of the Old Testament prophet is the apostolic circle (Peter, Paul and so on) who laid down authoritative teaching on the faith (see Eph 2:20; 2 Pet 3:2). Like an Old Testament prophet's words, such as Isaiah's, the apostle's teaching became part of the Bible. The apostolic circles were clear as to the unique authority of their position and teaching; see, for example, Paul in 2 Timothy 1:13, Jude in Jude 3, John in 1 John 1:1-4. Both the Old Testament prophet and the apostles in the New Testament were personally called by God (for example, Ezek 2:3-7). The revelation of God in the Bible (the teaching of the Old Testament prophets plus the apostles' teachings if you like) is, for the Christian, the final authority in all matters of faith and conduct.

Against that, the utterances of one holding the office of prophet in the New Testament church, such as Agabus in Acts 21:10, are thus subjective and non-authoritative by nature. Paul felt free to disobey them (see Acts 20:22; 21:4, 10-11) and certainly saw them as open to evaluation and testing (Acts 20:10-11; 1 Cor 14:29-30). Also, comparisons of Acts 21:11 with Acts 21:32-33 show us that they were not totally accurate. While in the Old Testament any false prophet was stoned to death, in the New Testament the prophet in the local congregation was simply open to correction and evaluation (1 Cor 14:29-30), implying that prophecy in the New Testament is of a different nature than prophecy in the Old Testament. It does not have the same authority as Scripture but is a continuing gift of insight that should be weighed against the Bible's authoritative teaching (1 Thess 5:19-21). In contrast to, say, the very individual call and national work of Jeremiah, the office of prophet in the New Testament church is given by God but also recognized by the church and subject to its local control and testing against Scripture's teaching.

Question 2. The aim of this question is to look at the effect of sin on the rest of society in Ezekiel's day. You may be able to discuss modern parallels in your own country, but try to avoid getting into a political argument! Encourage the group to think through how the actions of one group or class affect other people. For example, how does government corruption encourage ordinary people to be corrupt?

Question 3. The priests have deviated from the true faith in several ways (detailed in v. 26): they broke God's law, used things that were set apart for God (such as items in the temple) for pagan worship, lacked moral or theological discernment and blasphemed.

Question 5. The reference to prophets' "deeds" in verse 28 probably requires you to look back over the preceding verses to see which deeds are being "whitewashed" or disguised. Alternatively, they may be covering up their own misdeeds by claiming God's authority and inspiration for their actions when he had not spoken through them.

Question 7. This question will be a useful indicator as to how well the group has begun to understand intercession as a result of the studies to date.

Question 9. Some Christians believe all they can do is maintain their own spiritual lives and be fully involved in their churches. However, Christ's command in Matthew 5:13-16 to be salt and light calls us to be both a morally purifying influence in the world (salt) and a clear public witness (light). Much archaeological evidence indicates that the early church played a significant role in the public life of their communities. They prayed, evangelized and did good works, penetrating every aspect of their culture that was legitimate for a Christian to be involved in. Jeremiah told the exiles in Babylon to seek the welfare of the city in which they were in exile (Jer 29:7).

Question 10. Verse 30 only asks for a person to stand in the gap. The actions of a few can affect many. It should also be kept in mind that in countries where there are many Christians, great idolatry and materialism can and does exist.

Study 6. Praying for Everyone. 1 Timothy 2:1-8.

Purpose: To explore the importance of prayer in church life, and to review the studies so far.

General note. Questions 1, 4, 5, 7, 8 and 10 are "summary" questions, and you may want the group to look back at studies one through five as they respond. Accordingly, this study may take a little longer than usual. If you are using this study with a group, you may need to either (a) allocate more time for the study, (b) ask people to look at the study in advance and answer the questions numbered above on their own, with a view to everyone sharing their answers when the group meets together, or (c) split into two or three groups (if the group is large enough) and take two or three of the summary questions per group. Each smaller group can answer the questions and then share its answers with the rest of the group at the end of the meeting. For (b) or (c) to work you will really need more than one copy of the guide.

You may also want to have some summaries of the key ideas ready to share.

Question 1. One important dimension of prayer is intercession for leaders and the state. In Roman times prayers for the emperor and the officials showed Christians to be good citizens, demonstrating concern and respect, even though their primary allegiance was to Christ.

Question 3. Apart from showing no artificial division between truth and practice, Paul may be reminding his readers that God desires and commands evangelism, and they are to pray for all to learn of the good news of Christ. Note that verse 4 does not mean that everyone will become Christians; rather, God longs for all to come to accept what Christ has done for them, although many will not. Good doctrine—derived from good Bible knowledge and understanding—enables us to pray in accordance with God's will. The previous studies underlined how much God's promises were used as a basis for prayer.

Question 5. We should never consider ourselves superior to other people—saved or unsaved. The prayers of intercession studied so far show the intercessor caring for those under God's judgment, being willing even to perish that others might come to know Christ (see Paul's attitude in Rom 9:3).

Question 6. This is a difficult verse to interpret. Paul is probably implying that a socially peaceful environment (for example, where there is no civil war) is the best setting for the development of Christians' devotion, seriousness of purpose, attitude and character which is respected by nonbelievers. And he would hope that prayer for rulers would help bring this about. This does not mean to say, of course, that these qualities will not develop in other situations.

Question 9. Sin is a barrier to prayer (see, for example, Is 59:2; Jn 9:31). Disunity is a sign of sin, and unified prayer will not happen where Christians don't get together with each other. Lives also need to witness to Christ; if we teach about the love of Christ, the church must demonstrate it in its behavior. **Question 10.** See how many of the following qualities the group tracks down: perseverance (Dan 10:3); responsiveness to God's prompting (Gen 18:23; Ex 32:11; Neh 1:4; Dan 10:2); repentance (Dan 10:2; Neh 1:6); willingness to take risks (Gen 18:30; Ex 32:10-11; Neh 1:11); courage (Gen 18:27; Ex 32:11; Neh 2:2-3); self-sacrifice (Dan 10:3); in-depth biblical knowledge and application (Gen 18:25; Ex 32:11; Neh 1:8-10); identity with the sin of the people (Neh 1:6); concern for God's glory and reputation (Gen 18:25); intimate relationship with God (Gen 18:22; Ex 31:18; Dan 9:22, 23); humility before and fear of God (Gen 18:27, 32; Neh 1:5; Dan 10:12, 19); concern for others (Gen 18:23); integrity (Ezek 22:26; Dan 10:10); obedience to God's laws (Ezek 22:26); faithfulness to God's truth (Ezek 22:26), preparedness to take practical action (Neh 2:5; Ezek 22:30).

Now or later. If you carry out this exercise this as a group, you may discern how people's prayer lives have changed over the weeks you have been studying together. Bear in mind that instant change may not happen, but in these studies and by praying together for each other's prayer lives you can help each other begin the process.

Study 7. Relying on God. Psalm 5.

Purpose: To examine how we should pray when under pressure.

Group discussion. Encourage the group to explore *why* they react as they do in such circumstances. Christians may become discouraged when they face opposition or pressure (particularly when new to the Christian faith). However, these are times when we can learn much about God and his faithfulness. You may want to broaden the discussion to how these things affect other aspects of discipleship. **Question 2.** David in fact prayed both morning and evening (Ps 3—4). We need to be careful not to fall into legalism in thinking that failing to pray twice a day will make us less acceptable to God or that we can only pray at certain times of the day. However, in-depth, daily conversations with God were the practice of Daniel, David and, of course, Christ (who prayed for hours alone). Human relationships involve conversations both of many words and of few. Both are necessary in our relationship with God. Time deliberately set aside for solitary prayer is a crucial part of growing as a Christian. Many people find praying at the start of the day very helpful—to get the day in perspective and pray when they are least tired. **Question 4.** One example of what to look for is the way David addresses God

(v. 2). David writes as a king addressing a much greater king. David realizes that his acceptance by God is not based on his status, moral behavior or abilities. He can rely on God's mercy. See also verses 4, 7, 10 and 12.

Question 5. Discussions may remind you that Christians often fail to live as they should. The apostle John reminds us in 1 John that the mark of authentic Christian belief is not only correct doctrine but a life consistent with it.

Question 6. We can be confident of both the sovereignty of God over those who do evil and the ultimate justice of God in dealing with them. We know the evildoers will receive a just reward for their wrongdoing, even if evil *appears* to succeed.

Questions 7-8. Note references in the passage to God's moral view of evil (v. 4), his practical opposition to it (v. 10) and his comfort of the believer during persecution (v. 11). The apostle John says that in God "there is no darkness at all"(1 Jn 1:5). If God is perfect he can do no wrong; he is sinless. This does not mean, however, that God does not "regret" evil things happening; for example, he "regrets" profoundly that we ever rebelled against him, but it is not his fault. God is sovereign over and responsible for the universe, but he cannot be blamed for its sin and evil. He has, of course, supremely conquered it on the cross and on the last day will remove all trace of evil.

Question 9. Remember that the promise that God will shield us (v. 12) does not necessarily mean that we will never get hurt or experience suffering; however, the pain or suffering will never be greater than we can bear, and it only happens with God's permission. Our bodies and minds may suffer, but our relationship with God is secure.

Study 8. Being Honest with God. 1 Samuel 1.

Purpose: To understand that God is both interested in and responsive to prayers about our personal circumstances and needs, and to explore how he uses the suffering of an individual to bring about his wider purposes.

Background note. This story is set around 1100-1050 B.C., at the end of the period during which Israel was ruled by judges. The nation was in considerable moral and spiritual decline. Out of the human need and difficulty of a family situation, God brought into being Samuel, who became a judge of Israel as well as the prophet who anointed its first king.

Don't read any significance into the fact that both the prayers of women in these studies are connected with the subject of children. The Bible has more prayers by women than most people imagine. The book of Esther and the song of Deborah (Judg 5) are omissions I regret; they are not included only because they did not cover the subject material under consideration here.

Group discussion. Some Christians find it very hard to believe that suffering can in any way be positive, especially while experiencing it. However, such times may be when we are most open to hear God. Try not to let the discussion drift into a general debate on suffering.

Question 1. Verse 3 seems to indicate consistent worship, in comparison to the priests of the day who were leading scandalous lives (1 Sam 2:12-17). Someone in the group may pick up on the fact that Elkanah had two wives and see this as inconsistent with godly living. (Abraham, too, had concubines and secondary wives such as Hagar.) While this was recognized as legal in Deuteronomy (presumably as a concession to cultural pressures), Genesis originally recognized one wife (monogamy) as the norm, and this is reflected throughout the Scriptures. God still appears to recognize Elkanah and Hannah as godly people, despite this deviation from biblical standards. It appears that God chose, in this instance, to bring about his purposes through believing parents and that Elkanah and Hannah were appropriate people to parent Samuel.

Question 3. The group might find it helpful to imagine themselves in Hannah's situation and the conflicts she might have felt. Does she want a child to please herself, to please Elkanah, to please God or to spite Peninnah? Hannah clearly suffers greatly in her infertility, such that she cannot be comforted (v. 8). It would be reasonable to assume that she feels great conflicts about her desire for a child. Yet she does not allow bitterness or resentment to mar her relationship with God or stop communicating with him.

Some think we cannot pray to God unless we have entirely pure motives. Perfection of motives or any other aspect of life is not achievable this side of heaven. The important thing is that we seriously aspire to be like Christ and long to be holy. Despite the highest motives, we live with the reality that even if we desire and work to discover God's will in our hearts and minds, our motives will not be absolutely pure. Remind the group that Jesus himself experienced conflict in prayer between his will and God's will (yet, of course, without sin; see Lk 22:42). The most important way of dealing with impure motives or wrong reasons for praying is to confess them to God, asking him to forgive and to help us change. Useful further references on this issue include Luke 18:9-14; Romans 8:26-27; James 1:5; 1 John 5:14-15.

Question 5. Many factors can limit our honesty with God. We may think he is not interested; we may be frightened of him or think he is emotionless and unfeeling. Encourage the group to examine afresh such fears or inhibitions in the light of what we know about the character of God in the Bible and how Christ's death enables us to know forgiveness and experience his love personally.

Question 7. Look particularly at verses 11, 22 and 25-28. Hannah's son was not hers for selfish pleasure, but a gift from God to be offered in the service of God, as should be everything we have. The reference to the vow in verse 11 implies that she saw the child as separated out for or consecrated to God, symbolically represented in Hannah's culture by his hair not being cut. A similar concept is referred to in Numbers 6 and Judges 13:5. Hannah's faithfulness to God was later rewarded (see 1 Sam 2:18-21).

A parallel event concerning a parent giving up their child to God is recorded in the story of Abraham in Genesis 22; there God was testing Abraham to see if he trusted God to fulfill his promise. It is nothing to do with child sacrifice.

Question 8. John White comments: "The same pain that produced a Samuel to transform Israel, produced a transformed Hannah. If we could have talked with her ten years after the birth of Samuel (long before Samuel became a national figure) we would have found that she had never ceased to sound the praises of the God who had "tormented" her. She would laugh at the pain. Laugh at it not only because God had answered her but because pain had driven her into the arms of God. . . . Hannah was not a pawn in God's historical chess game. God's purposes for Hannah might have involved pain. But his larger purpose for Israel was linked with a loving purpose for Hannah" (*Daring*, pp. 88-89).

Question 9. A number of factors may have affected her: for example, the encouragement and blessing of Eli, who had initially misinterpreted her; the relief of being able to explain her feelings to God; a subjective sense of assurance after having prayed; or possibly her past experience of answered prayer giving her confidence that God had heard her. She addresses the Lord as the "LORD Almighty" in verse 11, a term which acknowledges God to be infinite and all-powerful.

Question 10. Their behavior, by taking Samuel to the temple, was consistent with what Hannah had promised they would do. She played her part in faithfully fulfilling her own promises made at prayer—namely, that the boy would be consecrated to God.

Question 11. Hannah may not at the time have understood her prayer to be prompted by God, but verse 5 makes it clear that her childlessness was because of the Lord's action. She prayed because she was childless, so her prayer was ultimately prompted by God.

Now or later. If you are using this study guide in a group, you will need to decide whether to meditate silently together as a group or individually. First Samuel 2:1-10 is a song expressing Hannah's confidence and trust in the God whom she worshiped and who had answered her prayer. Even having given her son back to God after waiting so long for him, she could praise God.

Study 9. Thanking God. Luke 1:46-55.
Purpose: To study the importance of thanking God and its place in our prayer life.
Question 1. The view we have of God will shape the way we see ourselves
and how we talk to God. Mary refers particularly to three aspects of his character—holiness (v. 49), power (v. 52) and mercy (v. 54).
Question 3. In verses 46-47 do not read any significance into the technical
difference between *soul* and *spirit.* The use of the different words owes more
to the structure of the poetry in the original language than to any intended
difference of meaning or function.

You may need to explain the meaning of the words *glorify* and *rejoice* to be
able to get the most out of the question. To glorify the Lord involves giving
praise to God for his actions and who he is—honoring and respecting him—
which should be done in words, attitudes and deeds. To rejoice involves
praising God and expressing our thanks to him. It would be a useful exercise
when preparing this study to look up other uses of the two words in the Bible
using a concordance. If time permits, encourage the group to think about not
just the words they use but also their attitudes when they express thanks to
God. We can say thank you without really meaning it!
Question 4. In popular usage *fear* means "terror." Fear in this sense is a
legitimate reaction to God because of his anger about our sin. However,
knowledge of the love of God in Christ saves us from the consequences of
sin and judgment. We need not be terrified of God if we rely on what Jesus
did on the cross to make us right with God. True fear of God is therefore
based on respect and reverence. At the same time Christians can forget that
he is the great and all-powerful God and be flippant with him. It is important for us to fear God in the right sense in order to pray with the correct
attitude. A right fear of God leads to his mercy and blessing being known
and experienced and God being allowed to be who he is, not limited by who
we think he is.
Question 5. Often our prayers concentrate on our personal spiritual experience and lack a breadth of vision of what God has done and is doing. Mary
could have only prayed about the Christ she was to bear (and she does in
vv. 48-49). But she also thanks God for a whole range of other things that
he has done in verses 50-55. She is not narrow-minded, so her prayer is
richer. The deeper our understanding of the Bible, the bigger our understanding of God.
Question 6. Helping the friend to look outside of their situation and to see

what God has done should help them to get their own circumstances in perspective. To see how God has worked in history helps us see how he can and
will work in the situations we face. Practically, we can pray with them to help
them talk to God.

Question 7. It is easy for Christians to harbor attitudes that God has con-
demned. Sin in our lives will undermine our prayer lives. Pride, arrogance
and preoccupation with wealth, status or power can render us unable to
thank God, appreciate him or serve him. What Mary describes is both a warn-
ing and simultaneously an encouragement to us. God's ultimate purposes are
not stopped by human sin.

Question 8. Mary's knowledge of how God had fulfilled his promises enabled
her to thank God for what he had done. Similarly the Bible should fuel our
prayers.

Question 9. This question is designed to help the group think about how balanced their prayer lives are. Some Christians spend all their time telling God
how wonderful he is but never intercede for others. Some always pray for
others but never thank God or pray for themselves. Our prayer lives need to
reflect the scope of biblical prayer—for example, intercession for others and
the world, thanksgiving, praise, repentance, asking for forgiveness, listening
to God and bringing God our personal needs.

Study 10. Blessing Other People. Ephesians 1:15-23; 3:14-21.
Purpose: To explore how we should pray for other Christians.

Background note. This letter was probably written for a wider group of
Christians than the church at Ephesus and circulated around several
churches in Asia Minor. Paul's priorities seem to have been to (1) reassure
believers who they were in Christ, (2) remind them what was available to
them in Christ and (3) instruct them how they should live together despite
their different backgrounds.

The book contains two prayers, and the two passages we look at give us an
understanding of how Paul prayed for the Christians he knew.

Group discussion. This is designed to get the group thinking about what
they want most for people. Is our highest desire for non-Christians that they
see Christ and know him? And for Christians that they become more like
Christ? If so, how do we pray for this?

Question 2. If the group finds this a difficult question, the following structure may help to give you a basis to start from.

☐ Paul gives thanks for their faith (1:15-16).

☐ Paul prays that the believers might fully experience what God has done for them (1:17-19).

☐ Paul focuses on God's power (1:19-23).

☐ Paul prays for the strengthening of the believers (3:16-17).

☐ Paul concentrates on the limitless love of God (3:17-19).

Question 3. Under the inspiration of the Holy Spirit, Paul's prayer arises out of the truths expressed in 1:3-14. Get the group to read 1:3-14, but make sure you concentrate on how Paul's prayer flows out of the truths in it. Don't get sidetracked on discussing 1:3-14 itself. Using the Bible helps us to ensure our prayer is in line with God's will and enables God to speak to us and guide or correct us as we pray.

> Prayer is a fire which needs fuel to burn and a match light it. If the fire burns low, we can fan it so that the flame may burn more fiercely. But all the fanning in the world cannot create a bonfire from a single match nor from a pile of dead, cold fuel.
>
> Fire must come from above; indeed it has already come. The Holy Spirit burns quietly within the Christian ready to light the fuel of Scripture's truth. But the fuel must be there. (*Daring*, p. 128)

Paul grounds his prayer in biblical truth about Christ, specifically God's choice of us to know him ("election") in 1:4-6, the fact that now we experience God's adoption of us into his family (1:5-8) and the future blessing of being one with God (1:9-10). Finally, Paul underlines how these blessings are true for each believer, Jew or Gentile, in 1:11-13.

Question 4. An example might be using the New Testament's teaching on the qualities expected of leaders and praying for local church leaders along those lines.

Question 5. Paul reminds us in 2 Corinthians 5:16 that we can no longer look at people from a worldly point of view; we must see those around us as Christ does and treat them accordingly.

Question 6. Encourage the group to put themselves in the position of the people Paul prayed for, and see if they can imagine what would have happened to them when Paul's prayers were answered.

For the second part of the question, have the group rewrite Paul's prayer as if he had prayed it for a non-Christian friend rather than a church.

Question 7. Paul emphasizes the death and resurrection of Christ as the cornerstone of the Christian faith. Paul wants them to fully identify with and understand Christ so that the power of the cross is apparent in their lives.

Question 8. Note the parallel themes of understanding (for example, 1:17-18) and intimate depth of relationship (for example, 3:16-19) in the two prayers. Being a Christian was not just about correct doctrine but ultimately about being in a relationship with God through Christ. Francis Foulkes comments, "Paul was aware of a danger, especially in the churches of the Greek world, of a faith that depended simply on intellectual knowledge" (*Ephesians,* Tyndale New Testament Commentary [Grand Rapids, Mich.: Eerdmans, 1989], p. 112).

Question 9. Often people find it hard to accept that Christ loves them personally. They may understand intellectually the idea that he loves them but not be sure of it. The balance is to both know and live the truth. Remember that just because someone cannot feel Christ's love, that does not mean that Christ does not love them. If the group wants to talk this through in more detail, you may need to talk about it after the study is over.

Question 10. We can easily lose sight of God's ability to change situations and people that we see as unchangeable. Realism is important so that we don't have false expectations, but 3:20 inspires us to see God as bigger than the problems.

Question 11. Two issues will probably arise here: the attitudes we have toward other people that we pray for and the way our prayers might now change in the light of the teaching on prayer the group has received, whether from this study or more generally.

Now or later. If you are meeting with a group, you can pray for each other.

Study 11. Praying Together. Acts 4:23-31.

Purpose: To learn about unity in group prayer, the importance of understanding God's control over circumstances and how to pray when facing opposition.

Background note. The setting for the passage is Acts 3:1—4:22. Peter and John have been used by God to heal a cripple, and they then speak about Christ. The temple authorities imprison them overnight and try to stop them from teaching about Christ. Their response is, "We cannot help speaking about what we have seen and heard" (4:20). They are then released and return to their friends.

Group discussion. If members of the group do not pray with other people, it may be better to use the personal reflection question instead.

Question 2. It is not clear from the passage precisely how the church prayed together; it would be difficult for them to pray an identical prayer together without having planned it first. It may have been that they prayed sentence by sentence following someone who led the prayer, or that the prayer recorded is a summary. Regardless of the way they prayed together, the critical point is that they prayed from the strength of their unity. See also Acts 4:32.

The quotation in verses 25-26 is from Psalm 2.

Question 3. It's particularly difficult to be dishonest in open prayer to God; to pray together demands genuine unity. It also cements the aims of the group if all pray together, longing for God to be at work.

Question 5. The central issue is God's sovereignty (or ultimate control) over circumstances. This is illustrated by the Psalm 2 quotation, clearly identifying that God's purposes are not defeated by the political, military or legal powers of governments opposed to him. Indeed, God even used the unlawful crucifixion of Christ to bring about his purpose in history, namely, saving us. (However, note that Herod's and Pilate's actions were not forced on them—they chose to act as they did. God works out his plan in history without robbing men and women of their freedom.) The fact that the early church could see their persecution as potentially bringing about God's purposes meant they did not see persecution as an overwhelming threat. This must have affected their attitudes toward those who persecuted them, just as Christ prayed, "Father, forgive them, for they do not know what they are doing" (Lk 23:34).

Question 6. The believers clearly did not lose sight of the overall mission God had for them; interestingly, they did not pray for their personal protection but instead for boldness in witness.

Question 7. We can be surprised that God answers our prayers because sometimes deep within we don't actually believe he will or can! Here the dramatic way God answered was presumably a special indication of his power, to reassure the church. An earthquake was often understood in the Old Testament to indicate God's presence (Ex 19:18; Is 6:4).

Question 8. Our desire for an "experience" of God can be selfish. Rather than seeking God to be better equipped to serve him and witness to Christ, we may wish only to satisfy our own sense of spiritual well-being. The expression "filled with the Holy Spirit" may generate a debate as to what this means and why it occurs, and whether we should seek such experiences. Try to avoid getting into a complex discussion on this point. Whatever the experience of the believers in this situation, the net effect was a new empowerment for evangelism. This ties in precisely with the words of Jesus in Acts 1:8: "But you will receive power when the Holy Spirit comes on you; and you will be my witnesses in Jerusalem, and in all Judea and Samaria, and to the ends of the earth." In experience-oriented cultures we may need to guard against wanting God simply to be *only* our source of personal spiritual experience and gratification, rather than seeking his gift of the Spirit to make us and the church more Christlike and equip us to fulfill the Great Commission.

Question 9. The group might like to talk about its experience of praying together, or learning to pray together if it does not do so already. Experienced Christians often need to exercise self-restraint and give less confident Christians the freedom to pray, however stumbling their prayers might be. Big, impressive prayers from learned Christians don't usually help young Christians feel able to pray easily; instead, those used to praying with others need to be sensitive and encourage others in gentleness when they are learning to pray.

Study 12. Praying with Confidence. Luke 11:1-13.
Purpose: (1) To understand Jesus' instruction to us as to how we should pray; (2) to explore God's attitudes toward us and our prayers as described in some of the parables of Jesus; (3) to develop our understanding about persistence in prayer; (4) to learn about the way God answers prayer and (5) to learn more about his character.

Background note. This section of Jesus' teaching on prayer arises out of his disciples' request for teaching (11:1). Verses 2-4 include what most Christian traditions call the Lord's Prayer, which is also found in Matthew 6:9-13 in a slightly longer form. Since Jesus intended the prayer as a pattern, not a rigid formula, it is not surprising that he taught it more than once. This also explains the variation in wording between the versions recorded.

General note. Questions 8 and 9 are designed to help you summarize things learned from all the studies in this LifeGuide. You may need to lead the group study in a different way to get the most out of the study questions (see the general note in the leader's notes for study six).

Group discussion. Some of the points on which your group needs reassurance will be covered during the study. Note any issues raised that need discussion later.

Christians' difficulties with prayer are sometimes symptoms of problems in their relationship with God. If we have a wrong view of God, we may doubt (for example) that he hears our prayers or wants to answer them. Apart from Jesus' example to his disciples as to how to pray, he gave his followers practical teaching about prayer. Just as he taught about the character of God, he demonstrated the character of God in his life on earth to help us to understand and approach him. He wants us to have confidence in approaching God, but not arrogance.

Question 1. The following is a brief analysis of the key points in the Lord's Prayer: (1) "Father" implies intimacy with God, as a child would address his parent, enabling us to understand that we can talk to God with intimacy.

Despite who he is, he is approachable and sees us as his children. (2) "Hallowed" (NIV) means "made holy"; the phrase "hallowed be your name" means we should approach God with reverence, aware of his nature and character. Also, it suggests that God's name will be revered as holy by others if they see his character glimpsed in our lives. (3) "Your kingdom come" means that in the present those who pray should long to see Christ's rule realized in our lives, and they long for the future reality that Christ will finally come and ensure that his will is perfectly done. (4) The prayer then moves in verse 3 from a focus on God's character and the outworking of his purposes to a prayer for the provision of our daily needs ("daily bread"), emphasizing our continual dependence on God. This discourages us from being arrogantly self-reliant or forgetful of his constant provision. (5) The final part of the prayer (v. 4) demonstrates that we can confidently approach a merciful God for forgiveness, and in being forgiven find the grace of God to forgive others. (6) The closing request, "And lead us not into temptation" (NIV), does not mean that we ask God not to tempt us, for he does not tempt us to sin (Jas 1:13). Instead it implies that in our weakness we come to God, recognizing the temptations around us, to ask that we might be able to resist the temptations we face and so lead a holy life.

The framework this provides for us therefore involves intimacy, reverence, a longing for the outworking of God's purposes, dependence on God and desiring to live a holy life, resisting temptation in God's strength. Even if group members are familiar with the Lord's Prayer, they will find it helpful to look at it a little more closely.

Question 3. To provide food and hospitality to a visitor was expected practice in Jesus' culture. The friend probably lived in a one-room house, so to get up to provide the bread would have awakened the family. Because the first friend persists in asking, thereby demonstrating the seriousness of his need for bread, his request is answered.

Question 4. How prayers are answered is a complicated subject. The following may be helpful background information.

As with the parable of the widow in Luke 18, God is not being likened to a grudging friend, an unkind father or an unjust judge in the way that he answers our prayers. The parable says effectively, "If a human is like this, think how much kinder God is."

God responds to prayer not because he has to be pushed into it but because he wants to give to us and to use us in accordance with his will (v. 13; 1 Jn 5:14). The reference in verse 13 to the Holy Spirit implies that the gift of the Holy Spirit to us is God's "best" for us, because he is the one who makes real to us what Christ has done for us. (It is doubtful that Luke has used the expression here to refer to the dispensing of particular charismatic gifts.)

If the answer to our prayer is not what we expect, it is always a sufficient answer (see v. 8); we get what we *need*, not always what we want! God cannot sin; thus if he answers or does not answer prayer as we expected, it is not God who is wrong. Often we want answers to our prayers that satisfy us, rather than answers in line with God's will. We also have to bear in mind that the way God works never limits human free will. We may pray for a friend to become a Christian (and we should), but God will not force them to do so.

Verses 11-13 point out by implication that if we view God as an unkind father (rather than a perfect one) we will be frightened to ask him, so we will never receive. Our faith is therefore undermined by wrong attitudes. Then we may not receive because we never ask.

Question 5. Note that the words *ask, seek* and *knock* are continuous tenses, that is, they imply *constantly* asking, seeking and knocking. Also, the three words imply degrees of intensity. First you ask, then you seek, then you knock. The underlying issue is similar to that in verses 5-8: if we really seek God's will and want to see our prayer answered in line with his will, we should constantly pray. On these verses Leon Morris comments: "Jesus does not say and does not mean that, if we pray, we shall always get exactly what we ask for. After all, 'No' is just as definite an answer as 'Yes'. He is saying that true prayer is neither unheard nor unheeded. It is always answered in the way God sees is best" (*Luke* [Grand Rapids, Mich.: Eerdmans, 1988], p. 196).

Question 6. We have seen from other studies (for example, study four on Daniel 10) that prayer often involves spiritual warfare. Because of the importance of prayer in our relationship with God, Satan will do his best to undermine individual and group prayer. Group members can do practical things to help each other pray, for example, by meeting one-to-one with another person in the group to pray regularly.

Question 7. An alternative discussion question might be "How has this study changed your view of God?" This should help the group reflect on the character of God portrayed in the passage.

Question 8. This question should draw out whether we are praying in a selfish or imbalanced way.

Question 9. This question is designed to help the group recognize the variety in prayer.

Question 10. Try to make this as practical as possible, and don't set unrealistic goals. It's better to achieve several modest goals than fail to achieve an impossible one. Group members may need to meet in twos or threes to pray for other people—and each other—over the next few weeks, or the whole group could meet (perhaps over breakfast) to have more time to pray together.

David Healey has worked in student ministry in the United Kingdom and Ireland, and is now the communications manager of Intercontinental Church Society, a Church of England mission agency. He lives in Sutton Coldfield, United Kingdom, enjoys travel and photography, and is married to Aileen. They have two boys, Calum and Euan, and Dave's prayer for them is that they will be more faithful pray-ers than he is.

What Should We Study Next?

A good place to continue your study of Scripture would be with a book study. Many groups begin with a Gospel such as *Mark* (20 studies by Jim Hoover) or *John* (26 studies by Douglas Connelly). These guides are divided into two parts so that if twenty or twenty-six weeks seems like too much to do at once, the group can feel free to do half and take a break with another topic. Later you might want to come back to it. You might prefer to try a shorter letter. *Philippians* (9 studies by Donald Baker), *Ephesians* (11 studies by Andrew T. and Phyllis J. Le Peau) and *1 & 2 Timothy and Titus* (11 studies by Pete Sommer) are good options. If you want to vary your reading with an Old Testament book, consider *Ecclesiastes* (12 studies by Bill and Teresa Syrios) for a challenging and exciting study.

There are a number of interesting topical LifeGuide studies as well. Here are some options for filling three or four quarters of a year:

Basic Discipleship
Christian Beliefs, 12 studies by Stephen D. Eyre
Christian Character, 12 studies by Andrea Sterk & Peter Scazzero
Christian Disciplines, 12 studies by Andrea Sterk & Peter Scazzero
Evangelism, 12 studies by Rebecca Pippert & Ruth Siemens

Building Community
Christian Community, 10 studies by Rob Suggs
Fruit of the Spirit, 9 studies by Hazel Offner
Spiritual Gifts, 12 studies by Charles & Anne Hummel

Character Studies
David, 12 studies by Jack Kuhatschek
New Testament Characters, 12 studies by Carolyn Nystrom
Old Testament Characters, 12 studies by Peter Scazzero
Women of the Old Testament, 12 studies by Gladys Hunt

The Trinity
Meeting God, 12 studies by J. I. Packer
Meeting Jesus, 13 studies by Leighton Ford
Meeting the Spirit, 12 studies by Douglas Connelly